Venetian	*French*	*Dutch-English*		
a *a*	a *a*	a *a*	a *a*	a *a*
b *b*	b *b*	b *b*	b *b*	b *b*
c *c*	c *c*	c *c*	c *c*	c *c*
d *d*	d *d*	d *d*	d *d*	d *d*
e *e*	e *e*	e *e*	e *e*	e *e*
f *f*	f *f*	f *f*	f *f*	f *f*
g *g*	g *g*	g *g*	g *g*	g *g*
h *h*	h *h*	h *h*	h *h*	h *h*
i *i*	i *i*	i *i*	i *i*	i *i*
j *j*	j *j*	j *j*	j *j*	j *j*
k *k*	k *k*	k *k*	k *k*	k *k*
l *l*	l *l*	l *l*	l *l*	l *l*
m *m*	m *m*	m *m*	m *m*	m *m*
Poliphilus	*Garamond*	*Caslon*	*Baskerville*	*Didot*

B I B L I O T O P I A

BIBLIOTOPIA

or, Mr. Gilbar's Book of Books &

Catch-all of Literary Facts & Curiosities

compiled by STEVEN GILBAR

decorations by ELLIOTT BANFIELD

DAVID R. GODINE · *Publisher*

BOSTON

First published in 2005 by
David R. Godine · *Publisher*
Post Office Box 450
Jaffrey, New Hampshire 03452
www.godine.com

LIBRARY OF CONGRESS
CATALOGING-IN-PUBLICATION DATA

Gilbar, Steven.
Bibliotopia, or, Mr. Gilbar's book of books & catch-all of literary facts & curiosities / compiled by Steven Gilbar ; decorations by Elliott Banfield.— 1st ed.

p. cm.

ISBN-13: 978-1-56792-295-0 (alk. paper)
ISBN-10: 1-56792-295-3 (alk. paper)

1. Books and reading—Miscellanea. 2. Literature—Miscellanea. 3. Bibliography—Miscellanea. 4. Books—Miscellanea. I. Title: Bibliotopia. II. Title: Mr. Gilbar's book of books & catch-all of literary facts & curiosities. III. Title.

Z1003.G47 2005
028'.9—dc22
2005013366

First Edition
PRINTED IN THE UNITED STATES OF AMERICA

PREFACE

Bibliotopia is virtually all around us. It is made up of libraries, bookshops, book clubs, reading groups, book reviews, literary Web sites, bibliophiles, bookworms, and common readers like you and me. Despite all the new and competing media, it happily continues to thrive in what has been termed the post-Gutenberg Galaxy. The miscellany of literary facts and curiosities that constitute this volume celebrates this world. You will find here all sorts of information – the significant and the trivial, the useful and the useless (but interesting, I hope) – arranged higgledy-piggledy so that you can dip in anywhere and be amused, edified, surprised, or all three at once. And it might turn you on to some new writers and books or inspire you to reread an old favorite. This book could not have quickened into being without the support of David Godine, defender of the faith that books matter and publisher of books that matter. As long as such friends of the book exist, literature will continue to flourish and have authority.

– STEVEN GILBAR

B I B L I O T O P I A

☐ ORIGIN OF "BOOK"

The word comes from *beech* because the ancient Saxons and Germans usually wrote runes on pieces of beechen board.

☐ DEVELOPMENT OF THE BOOK

The first books were fashioned on clay tablets. With the development of papyrus (the dried and split stems of a reedlike plant), scrolls displaced tablets. However, neither was suitable for the form of book that superseded them: the codex – a sheaf of bound pages. Clay was unwieldy and papyrus too brittle. The solution: parchment (made from fine animal skin) that could be cut into a variety of different sizes. Invented by the Pergamenes, it was called *pergamum*, or parchment, after the city. The parchment codex swiftly became the common form for books. By 400 A.D. the scroll had been all but abandoned, and books were being produced as gathered leaves in a rectangular form.

☐ INVENTION OF PAPER

In 405 A.D., Ts'ai Lun, a Chinese court official, began making paper from textile waste using rags. The technology spread to the Middle East. In the thirteenth century the Arabian-made paper and its method of production were exported to Italy, where hemp and linen rags were used. Paper completely replaced parchment in the nineteenth century with the invention of steam-driven paper-making machines, which used fibers from wood pulp to make paper. With the coming of the steam-driven printing press, wood-based paper transformed society: before then a book was a rarity and most people could not read. With the introduction of cheap paper, books, journals, and newspapers became available for nearly everyone.

☐ TREES INTO BOOKS

The typical tree makes about 11,500 pages of 8½ x 11-inch, 20-pound paper. One cord of hardwood produces about 943 100-page hardcover books.

◻ ORIGIN OF PUNCTUATION

The ancient scrolls used no punctuation, nor were words separated or any distinction made between upper- and lower-case letters. Punctuation is traditionally ascribed to Aristophanes of Byzantium (circa 200 B.C.) and was further developed by other scholars of the great Library of Alexandria.

◻ PARTS OF A BOOK

BOARD: A generic term for a stiff and thick paper.

BOOK BLOCK: The collated printed pages of a book, consisting of the leaves, or signatures, making up the unit to be bound.

CRASH: A coarse, open-weave, starched cotton material, used in edition binding for lining the spines of books.

DUST JACKET: A printed paper wrapper placed around a book for protection.

ENDPAPER or ENDSHEET: The plain, colored, fancy, or marbled paper attached to the inside of the board of a book after it has been covered. Endpapers serve as a structural bond between the case and the body of the book. Also called the "pastedown."

FLYLEAF: The free half of an endpaper, being the leaf or leaves not pasted to the boards, or covers, of the book.

FORE EDGE: The edge of a book opposite the spine. Sometimes called "front edge."

GUTTER: The adjoining inner margins of two facing printed pages, *i.e.*, the margin at the sewn fold of a signature.

HEAD: The margin at the top of a printed page.

HEADBAND: A decorative strip of woven material attached between the head and tail of the spine and the book block.

HINGE: The strip of fabric or paper placed between the two parts of library-style cloth-jointed endpaper, for the purpose of providing additional strength at the point of flexing.

JOINT: The exterior juncture of the spine and covers of a case-bound book.

LINING: A reinforcing strip applied to the spine of a sewn book, after gluing up, rounding, and backing, but before casing-in.

SIGNATURE: A single printed sheet of paper, folded and ready for collating, binding, and trimming.

SPINE: The collective fold-areas sections of a gathered book after sewing. Sometimes called "back."

SQUARE: The edge of the binding board or cover that extends beyond the book block.

TAIL: The lower or bottom edge of a book.

□ THE FRONT MATTER OF A BOOK

BLANK LEAF: An unprinted leaf at the beginning of the first signature or the end of the last signature to which the endpapers are attached.

HALF TITLE PAGE: The first printed page of a book, carrying only the title.

ADVERTISING CARD: A list of the author's works, sometimes limited to those issued by the publisher.

FRONTISPIECE: An illustration facing the title page.

TITLE PAGE: A page providing the full title, subtitle, authors (or other contributors), and publisher.

TITLE PAGE VERSO: Required information about copyright, edition, ISBN, etc.

DEDICATION PAGE: Identifies the person to whom the book is dedicated, if anyone.

TABLE OF CONTENTS: Sets out the parts and chapters of the book.

FOREWORD: Short introduction by a recognized authority.

PREFACE: Written by the author, it generally provides the rationale for writing the book.

INTRODUCTION: The author informs the reader what the book is about and how it might be used.

ACKNOWLEDGMENTS or PERMISSIONS PAGE: A listing of persons who assisted in preparing the book and individuals or institutions that allowed copyrighted materials to be reprinted in the book. May appear in the back matter instead.

QUOTATION PAGE or EPIGRAPH: A borrowed quotation that expresses the theme of the book.

BASTARD TITLE PAGE: A duplicate of the half title page, usually numbered page 1 of the main text.

CHAPTER OPENING: The beginning of the main text of the book.

□ THE BACK MATTER OF A BOOK

EPILOGUE: A short addition or concluding section, usually dealing with the fate of the characters.

NOTES: When not integated into the main text, usually arranged in chapter order.

APPENDIX: Additional information of value to the reader.

ADDENDUM: Material that supplements the main text.

GLOSSARY: An alphabetical list defining unfamiliar terms.

BIBLIOGRAPHY: A list of sources used in writing the book.

CONTRIBUTORS: Listed in back matter when not included in the acknowledgements section located at the front of book.

INDEX: An alphabetized listing of names, places, and subjects in the book that gives for each item the page on which it may be found.

COLOPHON: A statement crediting the typeface, printer, binder, and (possibly) designer and stating the limitation of the edition, if any.

□ SOME TYPES OF BINDING

ADVANCE READING COPY: Trade paperback versions of books released to book industry insiders prior to the book's official release date.

BOARD BOOK: Usually a children's book, the pages being made from sturdy cardboard to withstand rough use.

HARDCOVER or TRADE CLOTH: A book bound in cloth (or paper) over boards.

LIBRARY BINDING: A sturdy hardcover binding meant to withstand long-term use, usually without dust jacket.

MASS-MARKET SOFTCOVER: A smaller paperback, printed in large editions on cheap paper, like those commonly found at supermarkets.

PAMPHLET: A small work, often stapled, generally bound in a stiff paper wrapper.

SLIPCASE: A cardboard case covered in paper, cloth, or leather that houses a book, leaving only its spine exposed.

SPIRAL BINDING: A continuous metal or plastic cord binding often used for workbooks or other "how-to" books.

TRADE PAPERBACK: A book printed at the same size and on the same quality paper as a hardcover, but bound in stiff paper.

UNCORRECTED PROOF: Trade paperback similar to the advance reading copy, but not released for marketing purposes.

☐ FIRST CLOTH BINDING

The English publisher William Pickering was the first to replace the more costly leather binding with cloth in his Diamond Classics of 1822.

☐ BOOK SIZES

Atlas folio	up to 25″ tall
Elephant folio	up to 23″ tall
Folio	up to 15″ tall
Quarto (4to)	up to 12″ tall
Octavo (8vo)	up to 9¾″ tall
Duodecimo (12mo)	up to 7¾″ tall
16mo ("sixteenmo")	up to 6¾″ tall
24mo	up to 5¾″ tall
32mo	up to 5″ tall
48mo	up to 4″ tall
64mo	up to 3″ tall

☐ SOME IMPORTANT DATES IN PRINTING HISTORY

1438: Around this date Gutenberg worked on a plan to break out of printing texts using wood blocks. He set about carving individual letters, and developing a method to cast single letters in pieces that varied in width but were precisely the same height. He then built precision molds for casting the letters in lead. These letters were positioned in a "chase," which aligned and blocked the type on a modified wine press – the first recorded printing press.

1458: Nicolas Jenson, a French engraver working in Italy, began to develop types that merged rounder and more open Roman capitals with the rotunda letterforms preferred by Italian humanists to Gutenberg's black-letter (or textura) types. Still more important was the type he developed for his 1470 edition of Eusebius, which combined Roman capitals with lower-case letters derived from the chancery hand and which qualified him as the creator of the first pure "roman" type.

1476: William Caxton, an Englishman employed by the Duchess of Burgundy to translate French literature into English, is believed to have learned the art of printing in Cologne. He became intent on bringing the publishing arts to England. Around 1476 he produced and printed *The Dictes or Sayinges of the Philosophres*, the first book to be printed on English soil, and went on to open the first printing house in England.

1492: Aldus Manutius set up the first publishing company. His profitable innovation published in quantity books that were smaller and easier to hold and read. He applied a new format to printed books producing clearer, more open pages with wide, unprinted margins. His interest in the profitability of books fired his demand for well-edited volumes that all people would want to read, and which could be produced in the most affordable way. His typefaces influenced the industry throughout Europe through some twelve hundred published book titles.

1530: Claude Garamond was a punch cutter working in the printing business in France. His attention to detail and his skills in punch cutting produced type characteristics that worked better than any previously seen. His types became sought after by the better printers of the times. He established the first type foundry – a business set up specifically to market type to printers. In the course of this enterprise, he was able to liberate the printed page from its historic allegiance to calligraphic letterforms, a major step toward the evolution of modern type forms. The classic old style face that bears his name is ranked among the best in all typographic history.

1725: William Caslon spent his youth as an apprentice, journeyman, and master in metal tooling. His specialty was gun-barrel engraving. He went on to build his own type foundry by developing his own variations on Garamond's widely-imitated type styles. His types became so popular that in 1730 they were adopted as the standard for British newspapers. Caslon types were used for the first printings of the Declaration of Independence and the Constitution of the United States.

1730: As the printing industry grew to be an important segment of society, the eighteenth century saw many innovations and diversifications. John Baskerville, an English typographer and printer, was dissatisfied with the appearance of printed pages produced with technologies that had changed little since the time of Jenson. He also saw the profitability inherent in increased standardization of types and printing. In studying the legibility of existing types, he determined that lighter type forms were more legible at small sizes, an observation crucial to the printing in volume of smaller, less expensive books. Armed with this observation, Baskerville set out to develop types that were more and more independent of historical models. He developed not only his own type styles, but a new, more precise printing press that, along with his specially formulated inks, optimized the finer type style. More important, however, was his development of a new method for calendering paper, which yielded sheets far smoother than book papers of the day.

1780: Giambattista Bodoni, an Italian type designer and printer, admired Baskerville and his advancements in inks and papers. Bodoni was also heavily influenced by the work of the Didot family of typefounders and printers, which pushed Caslon's models to new extremes. But Bodoni was also an artist who aspired to produce types that were at once communicative and artistic. He went on to produce an extensive family of types – several dozen Latin alphabets, not to mention numerous non-Western faces – that would advance typography into the "modern" era of hairline serifs and heavy contrast between thick and thin strokes.

□ FIRST BOOK PRINTED IN EUROPE

The first book printed in Europe, the first Bible to be printed, and the first large book to be printed from movable metal type was the Gutenberg Bible, named after the inventor of movable metal type. It was printed in 1456.

□ FIRST BOOK PRINTED IN ENGLISH

The Recuyell of the Historyes of Troye translated and published by William Caxton in 1475.

□ FIRST PRINTING PRESS IN NEW WORLD

The first printing presses in the New World were established in Mexico City in 1533 and in Cambridge, Massachusetts, in 1638.

□ FIRST BOOK PRINTED IN AMERICA

The Bay Psalm Book (1640), a metrical translation of the Psalms by the ministers of the Massachusetts Bay Colony, was the first bound book printed in the English colonies.

□ FIRST BOOK ENTERED FOR COPYRIGHT

The Philadelphia Spelling Book was registered by its author, John Barry, on June 9, 1790.

□ ETYMOLOGY OF "LITERATURE"

Derives from *littera*, the Latin word for "letter."

☐ SOME PUBLISHING TERMS

ADVANCE: The sum paid to author in anticipation of royalty earnings.

AUTHORIZED: Written with the subject's consent.

BLURBS: Endorsements of the book by well-known writers or celebrities.

BOOK DOCTOR: A writer or editor hired by the author or publisher to improve a manuscript.

COPY EDITOR: Corrects grammar and spelling in a manuscript and checks facts for accuracy.

E-BOOK: A book published in electronic form that can be downloaded to computers or handheld devices.

ERRATA SLIP: A list of errors discovered after publication. Corrections are printed on a separate sheet and "tipped in" or otherwise attached to the book.

ERRORS AND OMISSIONS: Insurance available to authors concerned about possible lawsuits resulting from their work.

FIRST SERIAL RIGHTS: The right to excerpt a work in a periodical before publication.

FRONTLIST: Books that are about to be or have recently been published, as opposed to backlist title.

GALLEY: A bound edition of a work available for review and publicity purposes before publication.

GENRE: The sales category into which the title falls (*e.g.*, romance, how-to, mystery).

MID-LIST: A title or author that does not become a best-seller.

PRINT RUN: The number of copies produced in one printing.

PUB DATE: The scheduled release date for the book.

QUERY: A proposal letter from an author or agent.

RETURNS: Unsold copies returned by the bookstores or wholesalers to the publisher.

SUBSIDIARY RIGHTS: Sales of rights in the book for foreign publication, translation, first serial, film, book club, etc.

VANITY PRESS: A publisher who prints books at the author's expense.

□ ORIGIN OF "STEREOTYPE" & "CLICHÉ"

Originally a printing term, *stereotype* refers to a metal printing plate cast from a matrix that is molded from a raised printing surface, such as type. A *cliché* is a stereotype plate, from the French *clicher*, to stereotype (imitative of the sound made when the matrix is dropped into the molten metal to make a stereotype plate).

□ A BIBLIO- LEXICON

BIBLIOCLASM: The destruction of books.

BIBLIOGONY: The production of books.

BIBLIOKLEPT: A book thief.

BIBLIOMANCY: Divination by books.

BIBLIOMANIA: A rage for collecting books.

BIBLIOPEGY: Bookbinding as a fine art.

BIBLIOPHAGIST: A devourer of books.

BIBLIOPHILE: A book lover.

BIBLIOPHOBIA: A dread of books.

BIBLIOPOESY: The making of books.

BIBLIOPOLE: A bookseller.

BIBLIOTHECA: A library.

□ FIRST FORBIDDEN BOOKS INDEX

The Sacred Congregation of the Roman Inquisition published the first *Index of Forbidden Books* in 1559. It was revised for the final time in 1948.

☐ FIRST BOOK BANNED IN BOSTON

William Pynchon's *The Meritorious Price of Our Redemption, Justification, &c.* was banned in New England in 1650. A theological treatise, it was deemed to be heretical.

☐ THE FIRST AMERICAN BOOK CLUB

The Book-of-the-Month Club was established in 1926. The original judges were Heywood Hale Broun, Henry Seidel Canby, Dorothy Canfield, Christopher Morley, and William Allen White. The first selection to be distributed to the club's 4,750 members was *Lolly Willowes* by Sylvia Townsend Warner.

☐ OLDEST BOOKSTORE IN THE UNITED STATES

The Moravian Books Shop in Bethlehem, Pennsylvania, established 1775, is believed to be the longest-operating bookstore in the nation.

☐ THE MOST EVER PAID FOR A BOOK

An original four-volume subscription set of Audubon's *The Birds of America* sold at auction in 2000 for $8,802,500.

☐ THE MOST EVER PAID FOR A MANUSCRIPT

In 2004 an unfinished manuscript of Nathaniel Hawthorne's *The Scarlet Letter* was sold for $545,100 at auction by Christie's.

☐ ISBN

The ISBN (International Standard Book Number) is a machine-readable identification number. The modern computerized publishing industry is practically dependent on its use. It appears on the back cover of a book by the bar code.

☐ BIGGEST-SELLING BOOK OF ALL TIME

According to Guiness, the all-time best-selling copyrighted book is the *Guiness Book of World Records* which has sold ninety-five million copies since first launched in 1955.

☐ BIGGEST-SELLING CHILDREN'S BOOK SERIES

The Harry Potter series by J. K. Rowling has sold more than 250 million copies.

☐ LONGEST-RUNNING CHILDREN'S BOOK SERIES

The Bobbsey Twins (1904–72): seventy-two books.

☐ OLDEST BOOK FAIR IN THE UNITED STATES

New York Antiquarian Book Fair, established 1961.

☐ LARGEST BOOK FAIR IN THE WORLD

The Frankfurt Book Fair, with over ninety-five hundred exhibitors.

☐ THE READER'S BILL OF RIGHTS

The right to not read
The right to skip pages
The right to not finish
The right to reread
The right to read anything
The right to escapism
The right to read anywhere
The right to browse
The right to read out loud
The right to not defend your tastes

– from Daniel Pennac,
Better Than Life (1994)

J. K. ROWLING

☐ ILLITERACY

According to the UNESCO Institute for Statistics there are an estimated 862 million illiterate adults in the world, about two-thirds of whom are women.

☐ FIRST RAILWAY BOOKSTALL

W. H. Arnold & Son opened their first railway bookstall, at Euston Station in London, in 1848.

☐ WORLD'S LARGEST BOOKSTORE

Barnes & Noble is the largest bookstore chain and Amazon.com is the largest online-only bookstore. The largest single bookstore – 43,000 square feet – is Powell's Books of Portland, Oregon.

☐ OLDEST LIBRARY IN EXISTENCE

The Vatican Library, est 1451

☐ TEN LARGEST LIBRARIES IN THE UNITED STATES (BY NUMBER OF BOOKS)

1. Library of Congress
2. Harvard University Library
3. New York Public Library
4. Yale University Library
5. Queens Borough (New York City) Public Library
6. University of Illinois Library – Champaign/Urbana
7. University of California – Berkeley
8. The Public Library of Cincinnati and Hamilton County
9. Chicago Public Library
10. Free Library of Philadelphia

☐ FIRST PUBLIC LIBRARY IN THE UNITED STATES

Peterborough, New Hampshire, est 1833

☐ FIRST SUBSCRIPTION LIBRARY IN THE UNITED STATES

The Library Company of Philadelphia, est 1711

☐ OLDEST LENDING LIBRARY IN THE UNITED STATES

Redwood Library and Atheneum, Providence, R.I., est 1750

☐ TEN LARGEST LIBRARIES IN THE WORLD (BY NUMBER OF BOOKS)

1. Library of Congress
2. National Library of China
3. National Library of Canada
4. Deutsche Bibliothek (Germany)
5. British Library
6. Harvard University Library
7. Vernadsky Central Scientific Library (Ukraine)
8. Russian State Library
9. New York Public Library
10. Bibliothèque Nationale de Paris

☐ SOME LIBRARY TERMS

ABSTRACT: A brief summary of a book or article.

ACQUISITIONS: The department responsible for ordering of materials.

ANNUAL: A serial publication issued regularly once a year.

BACK NUMBER or BACK ISSUE: Any issue of a periodical older than the most recent issue.

CALL NUMBER: An alphanumeric code identifying an item in the library collection and indicating its location.

CARREL: An enclosed table for one reader.

CLOSED STACKS: Collections in which library staff retrieve requested items for users rather than allowing users to browse the shelves.

ENTRY: A single listing of a publication in a catalogue or index.

HOLD: A request that an item be kept for a patron until he can pick it up.

HOLDINGS: A library's collection of materials.

MONOGRAPH: Any published "real" book, as opposed to book-like objects such as a bound series of periodicals or photography albums.

NONCIRCULATING: Materials that may not be checked out by patrons.

SERIALS: Any publication issued in successive parts, usually at regular intervals and intended to be continued indefinitely.

STACKS: Rows of bookshelves in library.

ZEBRA NUMBER: The catalogue number from a bar code label used by the circulation department.

□ DEWEY DECIMAL SYSTEM

Most schools and public libraries use the Dewey system, a hierarchical classification system that divides humanity's knowledge, ideas, and artistic creations into ten major categories spanning a range from 000 to 999. Named for its inventor, Melvil Dewey.

- 000 Generalities
  - 010 Bibliography
  - 020 Library & information sciences
  - 030 General encyclopedic works
  - 040 Special topics
  - 050 General serials & their indexes
  - 060 General organizations & museums
  - 070 New media, journalism, publishing
  - 080 General collections
  - 090 Manuscripts & rare books
- 100 Philosophy & psychology
  - 110 Metaphysics
  - 120 Epistemology, causation, humankind
  - 130 Paranormal phenomena

- 140 Specific philosophical schools
- 150 Psychology
- 160 Logic
- 170 Ethics (moral philosophy)
- 180 Ancient, medieval, oriental philosophy
- 190 Modern western philosophy

200 Religion

- 210 Natural theology
- 220 Bible
- 230 Christian theology
- 240 Christian moral & devotional theology
- 250 Christian orders & local churches
- 260 Christian social theology
- 270 Christian church history
- 280 Christian denominations & sects
- 290 Other & comparative religions

300 Social science

- 310 General statistics
- 320 Political science
- 330 Economics
- 340 Law
- 350 Public administration
- 360 Social problems & services
- 370 Education
- 380 Commerce, communications, transport
- 390 Customs, etiquette, folklore

400 Language

- 410 Linguistics
- 420 English & Anglo-Saxon languages
- 430 Germanic languages (German)
- 440 Romance languages (French)
- 450 Italian, Romanian, Rhaeto-Romanic
- 460 Spanish & Portuguese languages
- 470 Italic languages (Latin)
- 480 Hellenic languages (Classical Greek)
- 490 Other languages

500 Natural science & mathematics

- 510 Mathematics
- 520 Astronomy & allied sciences
- 530 Physics
- 540 Chemistry & allied sciences
- 550 Earth sciences
- 560 Paleontology & paleozoology
- 570 Life sciences
- 580 Botanical sciences
- 590 Zoological sciences

600 Technology (applied sciences)

- 610 Medical sciences (medicine, psychiatry)
- 620 Engineering
- 630 Agriculture
- 640 Home economics & family living
- 650 Management
- 660 Chemical engineering
- 670 Manufacturing
- 680 Manufacturing for specific use
- 690 Buildings

700 The arts

- 710 Civic & landscape art
- 720 Architecture
- 730 Sculpture
- 740 Drawings & decorative arts
- 750 Paintings & painters
- 760 Graphic arts (printmaking & prints)
- 770 Photography
- 780 Music
- 790 Recreational & performing arts

800 Literature & rhetoric

- 810 American literature in English
- 820 English literature
- 830 Literatures of Germanic language
- 840 Literatures of Romance language
- 850 Italian, Romanian, Rhaeto-Romanic literatures
- 860 Spanish & Portuguese literatures
- 870 Italic literatures (Latin)

- 880 Hellenic literatures (Classical Greek)
- 890 Literatures of other languages

900 Geography & history

- 910 Geography & travel
- 920 Biography, genealogy, insignia
- 930 History of the ancient world
- 940 General history of Europe
- 950 General history of Asia (Far East)
- 960 General history of Africa
- 970 General history of North America
- 980 General history of South America
- 990 General history of other areas

□ LIBRARY OF CONGRESS CLASSIFICATION

A classification scheme devised for the Library of Congress now used by most research-level libraries in the United States. It is based on letters of the alphabet (allowing for a larger number of fundamental divisions of knowledge than the Dewey system) with subdivisions using letters, numerals, and decimal points.

A – General works
B – Philosophy, psychology, religion
C – "Auxiliary" sciences of history (heraldry, genealogy, general biography. . .)
D – History and area studies general and "old world"
E – History and area studies United States
F – 1–999: U.S. state and local history;
F – 1000+: other western hemisphere
G – Geography, anthropology, recreation
H – Social sciences
J – Political science
K – Law
L – Education
M – Music
N – Art and architecture
P – Language and literature

Q – Science
R – Medicine
S – Agriculture
T – Engineering, technology, crafts
U – Military science
V – Naval science

☐ TEN BOOKS ONE WOULD SAVE IN A FIRE

These are ten (if one could only save ten) books that Anna Quindlen wrote that she would save in How Reading Changed My Life *(1998).*

Pride and Prejudice by Jane Austen
Bleak House by Charles Dickens
Anna Karenina by Leo Tolstoy
The Sound and the Fury by William Faulkner
The Golden Notebook by Doris Lessing
Middlemarch by George Eliot
Sons and Lovers by D. H. Lawrence
The Collected Poems of W. B. Yeats
The Collected Plays of William Shakespeare
The House of Mirth by Edith Wharton

☐ SOME SUICIDES

Ryunosuke Akutagawa · John Berryman · Richard Brautigan · Paul Celan · Thomas Chatterton · Hart Crane · Stig Dagerman · Michael Dorris · Tristan Egolf · Sergei Essenin · Jesse Hill Ford · Charlotte Perkins Gilman · Spalding Gray · Carolyn Heilbrum · Ernest Hemingway · William Inge · B. S. Johnson · Yasunari Kawabata · Heinrich Von Kleist · Jerzy Kosinski · Primo Levi · Heather Lewis · Vachel Lindsay · Vladimir Mayakovsky · Walter M. Miller · Yukio Mishima · Breece D'J Pancake · Cesare Pavese · H. Beam Piper · Sylvia Plath · Anne Sexton · Sara Teasdale · Hunter S. Thompson · John Kennedy Toole · Marina Tsvetaeva · Virginia Woolf · Stefan Zweig

☐ SOME MEMORABLE OPENING LINES

"Call me Ishmael." – Herman Melville, *Moby Dick*

"Call me Jonah." – Kurt Vonnegut, *Cat's Cradle*

"'Take my camel, dear,' said my aunt Dot, as she climbed down from this animal on her return from High Mass."
– Rose MacAulay, *The Towers of Trebizond*

"It was a bright cold day in April, and the clocks were striking thirteen." – George Orwell, *1984*

"I write this sitting in the kitchen sink. That is, my feet are in it; the rest of me is on the draining-board, which I have padded with our dog's blanket and the tea-cosy."
– Dodie Smith, *I Capture the Castle*

"It was love at first sight." – Joseph Heller, *Catch-22*

"Last night I dreamt I went to Manderley again."
– Daphne Du Maurier, *Rebecca*

"In my younger and more vulnerable years my father gave me some advice that I've been turning over in my mind ever since."
– F. Scott Fitzgerald, *The Great Gatsby*

"On this Sunday morning in May, this girl who later was to be the cause of a sensation in New York, awoke much too early for her night before." – John O'Hara, *Butterfield 8*

"It is a truth universally acknowledged, that a single man in possession of a good fortune, must be in want of a wife."
– Jane Austen, *Pride and Prejudice*

"Hale knew they meant to murder him before he had been in Brighton three hours." – Graham Greene, *Brighton Rock*

"My name was Salmon, like the fish; first name, Susie. I was fourteen when I was murdered on December 6, 1973."
–Alice Sebold, *The Lovely Bones*

"I was born twice: first, as a baby girl, on a remarkably smogless Detroit day in January of 1960; and then again, as a teenage boy, in an emergency room near Petoskey, Michigan, in August of 1974." – Jeffrey Eugenides, *Middlesex*

"Whether I shall turn out to be the hero of my own life, or whether that station will be held by anybody else, these pages must show. – Charles Dickens, *David Copperfield*

"If you really want to hear about it, the first thing you'll want to know is where I was born, and what my lousy childhood was like, and how my parents were occupied before they had me, and all that David Copperfield kind of crap."
– J. D. Salinger, *The Catcher in the Rye*

"A screaming comes across the sky. It has happened before, but there is nothing to compare it to now."
– Thomas Pynchon, *Gravity's Rainbow*

"Happy families are all alike; every unhappy family is unhappy in its own way." – Leo Tolstoy, *Anna Karenina*

"Many years later, as he faced the firing squad, Colonel Aureliano Buendia was to remember that distant afternoon when his father took him to discover ice." – Gabriel García Márquez, *One Hundred Years of Solitude*

"I have been afraid of putting air in a tire ever since I saw a tractor tire blow up and throw Newt Harbine's father over the top of the Standard Oil sign." – Barbara Kingsolver, *The Bean Trees*

"My mother died today, or perhaps it was yesterday."
– Albert Camus, *The Stranger*

"It was the afternoon of my eighty-first birthday, and I was in bed with my catamite when Ali announced that the Archbishop had come to see me." – Anthony Burgess, *Earthly Powers*

"In our family, there was no clear line between religion and fly-fishing. " – Norman Maclean, *A River Runs Through It*

"Once upon a time, there was a woman who discovered she had turned into the wrong person."
– Anne Tyler, *Back When We Were Grownups*

◻ SOME PSEUDONYMOUS AUTHORS' REAL NAMES

Kobo Abe (Kimifusa Abe)
Anna Akhmatova (Anna Gorenko)
Sholem Aleichem (Solomon Rabinowitz)
Andrei Bely (Boris Bugaev)
Constantine Cavafy (Konstantinos Kavafis)
Paul Celan (Paul Antschel)
Maryse Condé (Maryse Boucholon)
Osamu Dazai (Shuji Tsushima)
Isak Dinesen (Karen Blixen)
Miles Franklin (Stella Franklin)
Maxim Gorky (Alexei Peshkov)
Knut Hamsun (Knut Pederson)
Yasmina Khadra (Mohammed Moulesschoud)
Halldór Laxness (Halldór Gudjónsson)
Pierre Loti (Julien Viaud)
Kamala Markandaya (Kamala Taylor)
Yukio Mishima (Hiraoka Kimitake)
Gabriela Mistral (Lucila Godoy y Alcayaga)
Alberto Moravia (Alberto Pincherle)
Pablo Neruda (Neftali Reyes)
Henry Handel Richardson (Ethel Richardson)
George Seferis (Georgios Seferiades)
Shchedrin (Mikhail Evgrafovich Saltykov)
Ignazio Silone (Secondo Tranquili)
Natsume Sôseki (Natsume Kinnosuke)
Italo Svevo (Ettore Schmitz)

◻ PEN/NABOKOV AWARD WINNERS

Started in 2000, the $20,000 prize is awarded biennially to an "international" author of "enduring originality and consummate craftsmanship."

2004 Mavis Gallant
2002 Mario Vargas Llosa
2000 William Gaddis

☐ SOME PARENT & CHILD WRITERS

Conrad Aiken: Jane Aiken Hodge
Kingsley Amis: Martin Amis
Robert Benchley: Nathaniel Benchley
James Lee Burke: Alafair Burke
John Cheever: Benjamin & Susan Cheever
Clive Cussler: Dirk Cussler
Nicholas Delbanco: Francesca Delbanco
Millicent Dillon: Wendy Lesser
Andre Dubus: Andre Dubus IV
Alexandre Dumas, *père*: Alexandre Dumas, *fils*
Richard Ellmann: Lucy Ellmann
Clifton Fadiman: Anne Fadiman
Constance Garnett: David Garnett
Moses Hadas: Rachel Hadas
Nathaniel Hawthorne: Julian Hawthorne
Frank Herbert: Brian Herbert
Stephen King: Owen King
Elizabeth Longford: Antonia Fraser
Anne McCaffrey: Todd McCaffrey
John McPhee: Martha McPhee
Rosamund Pilcher: Robin Pilcher
Anne Rice: Christopher Rice
Carl Sagan: Nick Sagan
Carolyn See: Lisa See
Michael Shaara: Jeff Shaara
Carol Shields: Anne Giardini
Susan Sontag: David Rieff
John Steinbeck: Thomas Steinbeck
William Makepeace Thackeray: Anne Thackeray Ritchie
Ernest Thompson: Anya Seton
Frances Trollope: Anthony Trollope
Evelyn Waugh: Auberon Waugh
H. G. Wells & Rebecca West: Anthony West
Laura Ingalls Wilder: Rose Wilder Lane
James Wright: Franz Wright
Charlotte Zolotow: Crescent Dragonwagon

☐ JERUSALEM PRIZE WINNERS

The Jerusalem Prize, Israel's top literary award (est 1963), is given every two years at the Jerusalem Book Fair to a writer whose work explores the freedom of the individual in society.

Antonio Lobo Antunes · Simone de Beauvoir · Sir Isaiah Berlin · Jorge Luis Borges · J. M. Coetzee · Don DeLillo · Max Frisch · Graham Greene · Zbigniew Herbert · Stefan Heym · Eugene Ionesco · Milan Kundera · Arthur Miller · V. S. Naipaul · Octavio Paz · Bertrand Russell · Ernesto Sabato · André Schwarz-Bart · Jorge Semprun · Ignazio Silone · Susan Sontag

---

☐ ON OUTDOOR READING

For a whole day together, have I lain
Down by thy side, O Derwent! Murmuring stream,
On the hot stones, and in the glaring sun,
And there have read, devouring as I read,
Defrauding the day's glory desperate.

– William Wordsworth

Then I went indoors, brought out a loaf,
Half a cheese, and a bottle of Chablis
Lay on the grass and forgot the loaf
Over a jolly chapter of Rabelais.

– Robert Browning

A Book of Verses underneath the Bough,
A Jug of Wine, a Loaf of Bread – and Thou
Beside me singing in the Wilderness –
Oh, Wilderness were Paradise enow!

– Omar Khayyam
(tr. Edward Fitzgerald)

Who is more happy, when, with heart's content,
Fatigued he sinks into some pleasant lair
Of wavy grass, and reads a debonair
And gentle tale of love and languishment?

– John Keats

☐ SOME LITERARY COUPLES

Diane Ackerman & Paul West
Elizabeth Barrett & Robert Browning
Ann Beattie & David Gates
Anne Bernays & Justin Kaplan
Caroline Blackwood & Robert Lowell
Jane Bowles & Paul Bowles
Geraldine Brooks & Tony Horwitz
Simone de Beauvoir & Jean Paul Sartre
Midge Decter & Norman Podhoretz
Joan Didion & John Gregory Dunne
Hilda Doolittle & Richard Aldington
Margaret Drabble & Michael Holroyd
George Eliot & George Henry Lewes
Louise Erdrich & Michael Dorris
Antonia Fraser & Harold Pinter
Tess Gallagher & Raymond Carver
Martha Gellhorn & Ernest Hemingway
Caroline Gordon & Allen Tate
Sue Halpern & Bill McKibben
Kathryn Harrison & Colin Harrison
Shirley Hazzard & Francis Steegmuller
Lillian Hellman & Dashiell Hammett
Gilbert Highet & Helen MacInnes
Brenda Hillman & Robert Hass
Gertrude Himmelfarb & Irving Kristol
Siri Hustvedt & Paul Auster
Shirley Jackson & Stanley Edgar Hyman
Pamela Hansford Johnson & C. P. Snow
Faye Kellerman & Jonathan Kellerman
Jane Kenyon & Donald Hall
Cassandra King & Pat Conroy
Nicole Krause & Jonathan Safran Foer
Gayle Lynds & Dennis Lynds ("Michael Collins")
Mary McCarthy & Edmund Wilson
Katherine Mansfield & John Middleton Murry
Margaret Millar & Ross Macdonald

Elsa Morante & Alberto Moravia
Anka Muhlstein & Louis Begley
Marcia Muller & Bill Pronzini
Iris Murdoch & John Bayley
Antonya Nelson & Robert Boswell
Sylvia Plath & Ted Hughes
Laura Riding & Robert Graves
Vita Sackville-West & Harold Nicolson
Alice Sebold & Glen David Gold
Mary Shelley & Percy Bysshe Shelley
Jane Shore & Howard Norman
Jean Stafford & Robert Lowell
Anne Streiber & Whitley Streiber
Dorothy Thompson & Sinclair Lewis
Claire Tomalin & Michael Frayn
Rose Tremain & Richard Holmes
Diana Trilling & Lionel Trilling
Avelet Waldman & Michael Chabon
Katharine S. White & E. B. White
Marianne Wiggins & Salman Rushdie
Kate Wilhelm & Damon Knight
Mary Wollstonecraft & William Godwin
Elinor Wylie & William Rose Benét
Helen Yglesias & José Yglesias
Marya Zaturenska & Horace Gregory

☐ SOME FS&G AUTHORS

In 1946 Roger W. Straus, Jr. (1917–2004) founded the publishing firm that would ultimately be known as Farrar, Straus & Giroux and become home to some of the most important writers of the second half of the twentieth century, including:

Joseph Brodsky · Colette · Carlos Fuentes · Shirley Hazzard · Seamus Heaney · Robert Lowell · John McPhee · Edna O'Brien · Flannery O'Connor · Grace Paley · Marilynne Robinson · Philip Roth · Isaac Bashevis Singer · Alexander Solzhenitsyn · Susan Sontag · Scott Turow · Mario Vargas Llosa · Derek Walcott · Edmund Wilson · Tom Wolfe

☐ SOME NOTABLE TRILOGIES

The New York Trilogy by Paul Auster
The Haitian Trilogy by Madison Smartt Bell
The Regeneration Trilogy by Pat Barker
The House of Earth by Pearl S. Buck
The Bebb Trilogy by Frederick Buechner
The Long Day Wanes by Anthony Burgess
The Deptford Trilogy by Robertson Davies
U.S.A. Trilogy by John Dos Passos
The Barrytown Trilogy by Roddy Doyle
The Studs Lonigan Trilogy by James T. Farrell
The Forsyte Saga by John Galsworthy
The Border Trilogy by Cormac McCarthy
The Cairo Trilogy by Naguib Mahfouz
The Balkan Trilogy by Olivia Manning
The New Mexico Trilogy by John Nichols
The Bounty Trilogy by Charles Nordhoff & James Norman Hall
The Country Girls Trilogy by Edna O'Brien
The Ohio Trilogy by Conrad Richter
The American Trilogy by Philip Roth
The Baroque Cycle by Neil Stephenson

☐ SOME AUTHOR EPONYMS

Baedeker: Karl Baedeker (1801–59)
Brechtian: Bertolt Brecht (1898–1956)
Byronic: Lord Byron (1788–1824)
Jamesian: Henry James (1843–1916)
Kafkaesque: Franz Kafka (1883–1924)
Machiavellian: Niccolò Machiavelli (1469–1527)
Masochism: Leopold von Sacher-Masoch (1836–1895)
Orwellian: George Orwell (1903–1950)
Petrarchan sonnet: Petrarch (1304–1374)
Platonic: Plato (c. 427 B.C.)
Rabelaisian: François Rabelais (1483–1552)
Sadism: Marquis de Sade (1740–1814)
Sapphic: Sappho (630–602 B.C.)

Shakespearean: William Shakespeare (1564–1616)
Shavian: George Bernard Shaw (1856–1950)
Spenserian stanza: Edmund Spenser (1552–1599)

◻ GREATEST ADVENTURE BOOKS

Book *magazine asked experts on adventure writing to vote for the fifty greatest adventure books ever. Here are the top ten:*

1. *The Odyssey* (c. 800 B.C.) by Homer
2. *Heart of Darkness* (1902) by Joseph Conrad
3. *Moby Dick* (1851) by Herman Melville
4. *The Worst Journey in the World* (1922) by Apsley Cherry-Garrard
5. *Don Quixote* (1605–15) by Miguel de Cervantes
6. *The Adventures of Huckleberry Finn* (1884) by Mark Twain
7. *Alice's Adventures in Wonderland* (1865) by Lewis Carroll
8. *Annapurna* (1952) by Maurice Herzog
9. *Robinson Crusoe* (1719) by Daniel Defoe
10. *Endurance* (1931) by F. A. Worsley

◻ FICTION GENRES

Action/Adventure · Sea stories · Chillers/Horror · Mystery/Thrillers/Suspense/Crime fiction · Family sagas · Historical novels · Romance · Sci Fi/Fantasy · Westerns · Graphic novels · Christian fiction · Children/Young Adult

---

◻ AUTHORS PRONUNCIATION GUIDE

Chinua Achebe: ah-CHAY-bay
Aesop: EE-sup
Yehuda Amichai: ya-HOOD-ah ahm-ih-KHI
Nina Berberova: bur-BEAR-uh-vuh
Jorge Luis Borges: HOR-hay lew-EES BORE-hays
Karel Čapek: KAH-rel CHAH-pek
Catullus: kuh-TULL-uhs
J. M. Coetzee: cot-TSEE-ah

MARCEL PROUST

Isak Dinesen: EE-sahk DEE-nuh-suhn
Seamus Heaney: SHAY-muhs HEE-nee
Søren Kierkegaard: SUUR-un KEER-kuh-gahrd
Milan Kundera: MEE-lun kun-DER-uh
Hanif Kureishi: ha-NEEF koor-EE-shee
Primo Levi: PREE-mo LAY-vee
Naguib Mahfouz: nah-JEEB mah-FOOZ
Farley Mowat: rhymes with "poet"
Kenzaburo Oe: OH-A
Ovid: AHV-uhd
Amos Oz: ahm-AHSS OZE
Fernando Pessoa: PES-wah
Leonardo Sciascia: SHA-sha
Henryk Sienkiewicz: shen-KYAY-vich
Josef Skvoresky: SHQUOR-st-skee
Wole Soyinka: WOH-leh Shaw-YIN-kah
Wislawa Szymborska: WEES-wava shim-BOR-ska
A. B. Yehoshua: yeh-HOH-shoo-ah
Xu Xi: shoe-SEE

□ WORLD'S LONGEST NOVEL

According to Guiness, Marcel Proust's thirteen-volume *A la recherche du temps perdu* (*In Search of Lost Time*) contains 9,609,000 characters (letters and spaces).

□ VOLUMES OF PROUST'S IN SEARCH OF LOST TIME

Swann's Way (or *The Way by Swann's*)
Within a Budding Grove (or *In the Shadow of Young Girls in Flower*)
The Guermantes Way
Sodom and Gomorrah (or *Cities of the Plain*)
The Captive (or *The Prisoner*)
The Fugitive (or *The Sweet Cheat Gone*)
Time Regained (or *Finding Time Again*)

☐ WORLD'S LARGEST BOOK PRIZE

Since 1996 the International IMPAC Dublin Literary Award has been given annually to a title nominated from libraries around the world. At a value of 100,000 Irish pounds, it is the world's richest literary prize for a single work of fiction.

2005: *The Known World* by Edward B. Jones
2004: *This Blinding Absence of Light* by Tahar Ben Jelloun
2003: *My Name Is Red* by Orhan Pamuk
2002: *Atomised* by Michel Houellebecq
2001: *No Great Mischief* by Alistair MacLeod
2000: *Wide Open* by Nicola Barker
1999: *Ingenious Pain* by Andrew Miller
1998: *The Land of Green Plums* by Herta Müller
1997: *A Heart So White* by Javier Marías
1996: *Remembering Babylon* by David Malouf

☐ SOME WRITERS WITH LAW DEGREES

Miguel Ángel Asturias · Louis Auchincloss · Francis Bacon · David Baldacci · Honoré de Balzac · William Barnhardt · Louis Begley · Edward Bellamy · Ugo Betti · James Boswell · William Cullen Bryant · Bartle Bull · John Burdett · Morley Callaghan · Stephen L. Carter · John Casey · Da Chen · Martin Clark · Octavius Roy Cohen · Cyrus Colter · Stephen Coonts · Jeffrey Deaver · Richard Dooling · Philip Friedman · John Galsworthy · Anne Giardini · Stephen Greenleaf · John Grisham · Frank Harris · Adam Haslett · Heinrich Heine · George V. Higgins · A. E. Hotchner · Roderic Jeffries · James Weldon Johnson · Nikos Kazantzakis · Philip Kerr · William Lashner · Gus Lee · Walter Lord · James Russell Lowell · Archibald MacLeish · James Alan McPherson · Carey McWilliams · Maurice Maeterlinck · Philip M. Margolin · Steve Martini · Edgar Lee Masters · Czelaw Milosz · Yxta Maya Murray · Pamela O'Shaughnessy · Richard North Patterson · Matthew Pearl · Charles Reznikoff · Kermit Roosevelt · Murray Schisgal · Sir Walter Scott · Lisa Scottoline · Wallace Stevens · Robert Louis Stevenson · T. S. Stribling · Scott Turow · Andrew Vachss · Lew Wallace

☐ LONGEST POPULAR NOVEL

Stephen King's *Dark Tower* series at more than four thousand pages

---

☐ NOBEL PRIZE (LITERATURE) REFUSALS

Jean-Paul Sartre (1964) The only honoree to turn down the prize voluntarily, he refused it on the grounds that such honors could interfere with a writer's responsibilities to his readers.

Boris Pasternak (1958) Pasternak was forced by the Soviet Government to refuse the Nobel Prize.

☐ SOME FAMOUS LITERARY ADULTERESSES

Emma Bovary (Gustave Flaubert, *Madame Bovary*)
Effi Briest (Theodor Fontane, *Effi Briest*)
Constance Chatterly (D. H. Lawrence, *Lady Chatterly's Lover*)
Francesca Johnson (Robert James Waller, *The Bridges of Madison County*)
Anna Karenina (Leo Tolstoy, *Anna Karenina*)
Luisa (José Maria Eça de Queiroz, *Cousin Basilio*)
Sarah Miles (Graham Greene, *The End of the Affair*)
Edna Pontelier (Kate Chopin, *The Awakening*)
Hester Prynne (Nathaniel Hawthorne, *The Scarlet Letter*)
Thérèse Raquin (Emile Zola, *Thérèse Raquin*)
Cora Smith (James M. Cain, *The Postman Always Rings Twice*)

☐ SOME NOTABLE QUARTETS

The Alexandria Quartet by Lawrence Durrell
Four Seasons Quartet by Maureen Howard
The Time Quartet by Madeleine L'Engle
The Earthsea Tetralogy by Ursula K. Le Guin
The Martha Quest Novels by Doris Lessing
The Berrybender Narratives by Larry McMurtry
The Girls by Henry de Montherlant
The Raj Quartet by Paul Scott
The Rabbit Tetralogy by John Updike

☐ LITERARY SIBLINGS

Joan Aiken & Jane Aiken Hodge
Donald Barthelme & Frederick Barthelme
Aimee Bender & Karen Bender
Anne Brontë, Charlotte Brontë & Emily Brontë
Susan Cheever & Benjamin Cheever
Nora Ephron & Amy Ephron
Margaret Drabble & A. S. Byatt
Antonia Fraser, Rachel Billington & Thomas Pakenham
Denis Hamill & Pete Hamill
A. E. Housman & Laurence Housman
Aldous Huxley & Julian Huxley
Henry James & William James
John Lehman & Rosamond Lehman
Frank McCourt & Malachi McCourt
Heinrich Mann & Thomas Mann
Susan Minot, Eliza Minot & George Minot
John Cowper Powys, Llewelyn Powys & T. F. Powys
Christina Rossetti & Dante Gabriel Rossetti
David Sedaris & Amy Sedaris
Isaac Bashevis Singer & I. J. Singer
Edith Sitwell, Osbert Sitwell & Sachaverell Sitwell
Alexander Theroux& Paul Theroux
Carl Van Doren & Mark Van Doren
Evelyn Waugh & Alec Waugh
Geoffrey Wolff & Tobias Wolff

☐ SOME WRITERS WHO DIED IN THEIR TWENTIES

Anne Brontë (29) · Rupert Brooke (28) · Stephen Crane (29) John Keats (26) · Comte de Lautréamont (24) · Mikhail Lermontov (27) · Novalis (29) · Wilfred Owen (25) Breece D'J Pancake (26) · Clere Parsons (23) · Raymond Radiguet (20) · Alan Seager (28) · Percy Bysshe Shelley (29) · Sir Philip Sidney (28) · George Trakl (27)

□ SOME GIVEN NAMES

S. Y. Agnon: Shmuel Czackes
Woody Allen: Allen Konigsberg
Maya Angelou: Marguerite Johnson
Piers Anthony: Piers Jacob
Toni Cade Bambara: Miltona Mirkin Cade
Amiri Baraka: LeRoi Jones
Saul Bellow: Solomon Bellows
Sandra Benitez: Sandy Ables
T. Coraghessan Boyle: Thomas J. Boyle
Paul Celan: Paul Antschel
Leslie Charteris: Leslie Yin
Joseph Conrad: Josef Korzeniowski
Rubín Dario: Félix Rubén García y Sarmiento
Joseph Epstein: Meyer Epstein
Fannie Flagg: Patricia Neal
Ford Madox Ford: Ford Hermann Hueffer
Robert Hayden: Asa B. Sheffey
Patricia Highsmith: Mary Plangman
Bell Hooks: Gloria Jean Watkins
Evan Hunter: Salvatore Lombino
Pico Iyer: Siddarth Pico Raghavan Iyer
Jan Karon: Janice Meredith Wilson
Anna Kavan: Helen Woods
Jack Kerouac: Jean-Louis Lebies de Kerouac
Jamaica Kincaid: Elaine Richardson
Jhumpa Lahiri: Nilanjana Sudeshna Lahiri
William Least Heat-Moon: William Trogdon
Harper Lee: Nelle Harper Lee
Cormac McCarthy: Charles J. McCarthy, Jr.
Armistead Maupin: Armistead Jones, Jr.
Rick Moody: Hiram F. Moody III
Jan Morris: James Morris
Toni Morrison: Chloe Anthony Wofford
Frederic Morton: Fritz Mandelbaum
Iris Origo: Margaret Cutting

Z. Z. Packer: Zuwena Packer
Jean Plaidy: Eleanor Hibbert
Harold Robbins: Harold Rubin
Sonia Sanchez: Wilsonia Driver
Evelyn Scott: Elsie Dunn
Ntozake Shange: Paulette Williams
Sam Shepard: Samuel Shepard Rogers VII
Tom Stoppard: Tomas Straussler
Studs Terkel: Louis Terkel
August Wilson: Frederick Kittel

☐ SOME UNFINISHED NOVELS

James Agee, *A Death in the Family*
Jane Austen, *Sanditon*
Joseph Conrad, *Suspense*
Charles Dickens, *The Mystery of Edwin Drood*
F. Scott Fitzgerald, *The Last Tycoon*
Gustave Flaubert, *Bouvard and Pécuchet*
Nathaniel Hawthorne, *Dr. Grimshawe's Secret*
Ernest Hemingway, *The Garden of Eden*
Henry James, *The Ivory Tower*
Franz Kafka, *Amerika*
D. H. Lawrence, *Mr. Noon*
Malcolm Lowry, *October Ferry to Gabriola*
Robert Musil, *The Man Without Qualities*
Georges Perec, *"53 Days"*
Marcel Proust, *Jean Senteuil*
Sir Walter Scott, *The Siege of Malta*
Stendhal, *Lamiel*
Robert Louis Stevenson, *Weir of Hermiston*
William Thackeray, *Denis Duval*
Thomas Wolfe, *The Hills Beyond*

☐ FIRST ACKNOWLEDGED AUTHOR

In 2300 B.C., the high priestess Princess Enheduanna addressed for the first time a "dear reader" in her songs.

☐ FIVE PENTALOGIES

Earth's Children by Jean Auel
The Danny O'Neill Pentalogy by James T. Farrell
The Lavette Family Saga by Howard Fast
The Once and Future King Series by T. H. White
The Hitchhiker's Guide to the Galaxy by Douglas Adams

☐ FIVE BOOKS OF MOSES

Genesis · Exodus · Leviticus · Numbers · Deuteronomy

☐ SOME OLD TESTAMENT TITLES

Ernest Hemingway *The Sun Also Rises*	The sun also riseth, and the sun goeth down; and hasteth to the place where he arose. – Ecclesiastes
Thornton Wilder *The Skin of Our Teeth*	I am escaped with the skin of my teeth. – Job
Stephen Fry *Moab Is My Washpot*	Moab is my washpot; over Edom will I cast out my shoe. – Psalms
D. H. Lawrence *Aaron's Rod*	And it came to pass, that on the morrow Moses went into the tabernacle of witness; and, behold the rod of Aaron for the house of Levi was budded. – Numbers
William Faulkner *Absalom! Absalom!*	O my son Absalom, my son, my son Absalom! Would God I had died for thee, O Absalom, my son, my son. – 2 Samuel
John Steinbeck *East of Eden*	And Cain went out from the presence of the Lord, and dwelt in the land of Nod, on the east of Eden. – Genesis
Edith Wharton *The House of Mirth*	The heart of the wise is in the house of mourning, but the heart of fools is in the house of mirth. – Ecclesiastes

Mark Helprin *Refiner's Fire*	But who may abide the day of his coming? And who shall stand when he appeareth? For he is like a refiner's fire, and like fullers' soap. – Malachi
Henry James *The Golden Bowl*	Or ever the silver cord be loosed, or the golden bowl be broken.... Then shall the dust return to the earth as it was: and the spirit shall return unto God who gave it. Vanity of vanities, saith the preacher; all is vanity. – Ecclesiastes

---

◻ SOME BIBLICAL CLICHÉS

Some expressions from the Good Book have become so shopworn as to become clichés – at least according to Eric Partridge (1894-1979), the English language maven.

The apple of one's eye (Psalms)
Balm in Gilead (Jeremiah)
The bottomless pit (Revelation)
Cast into the outer darkness (Matthew)
Cast one's bread upon the waters (Ecclesiastes)
Cast pearls before swine (Matthew)
Cloud of witnesses (Hebrews)
Enemy at the gate (Psalms)
A fly in the ointment (Ecclesiastes)
Gall and wormwood (Lamentations)
Go down to the sea in ships (Psalms)
Hide one's light under a bushel (Matthew)
The law of the Medes and Persians (Daniel)
A man after his own heart (Samuel)
Their name is Legion (Mark)
The race is to the swift (Ecclesiastes)
Sackcloth and ashes (Matthew)
To suffer fools gladly (Corinthians)
The wages of sin (Romans)
Weighed in the balance and found wanting (Daniel)

☐ SOME (POSSIBLY) BIPOLAR WRITERS

Hans Christian Andersen · Honoré de Balzac · Charles Baudelaire · William Blake · Emily Dickinson · T. S. Eliot · William Faulkner · F. Scott Fitzgerald · Ernest Hemingway · Hermann Hesse · Victor Hugo · John Keats · Sylvia Plath · Edgar Allan Poe · Mary Shelley · William Styron · Alfred, Lord Tennyson · Walt Whitman · Virginia Woolf · Emile Zola

---

☐ SOME CURIOUS LITERARY WORDS

ANALECTS: A collection of writings.

APOLOGUE: A moral fable or allegorical story.

BOWDLERIZE: To remove "objectionable" passages from a book.

CHRESTOMATHY: A collection of choice literary passages.

CORRIGENDUM: A mistake to be corrected, especially an error in a printed book.

ENCHIRIDION: A book carried in the hand for reference.

ENCOMIUM: High praise given in speech or writing.

EPOPEE: Epic poetry.

EXEGESIS: A critical exposition of a text.

FASCICLE: One section of a book that is published in installments.

FACETIÆ: Humorous writings.

HAGIOGRAPHY: The writing of the lives of saints.

HEPTASTICH: A stanza or strophe consisting of seven lines.

HERMENEUTICS: Methodology of interpretation, especially of scriptural text.

JEREMIAD: A lamentation.

LUCUBRATION: A literary work, especially one of pedantic or elaborate character.

MONOGRAPH: A scholarly book or a treatise on a single subject, class of subjects, or person.

PANEGYRIC: A piece of writing praising a person or thing; a tribute.

PICARESQUE: Fiction dealing with the adventures of a rogue.

POETASTER: An inferior poet.

PROLEGOMENON: The introductory essay in a book.

RUBRIC: A heading of a chapter, section, etc.

SCHOLIAST: Annotator or commentator on the classics.

SCREED: A long and dull piece of writing.

SESQUIPEDALIAN: A writer who uses long words.

VARIORUM: With notes of various editors or commentators or with various versions of a text.

☐ SOME NOVELS IN VERSE

Aniara by Harry Martinson
Autobiography of Red by Anne Carson
Bloodlines by Fred D'Aguilar
Darlington's Fall by Brad Leithauser
The Emperor's Babe by Bernardine Evanisto
Eugene Onegin by Alexander Pushkin
The Golden Gate by Vikram Seth
Human Landscapes from My Country by Nazim Hikmet
Pale Fire by Vladimir Nabokov
Rip Tide by William Rose Benét
The Wild Party by Moncure March

☐ SOME TYPES OF POEMS

AMPHIGORY: A poem that makes no sense.

AUBADE: A poem written to celebrate the dawn.

BALLAD: A poem that tells a story.

DITHYRAMB: A Greek lyric poem honoring Bacchus.

ELEGY: Usually laments the death of a person.

EPIC: A long poem, usually about a heroic figure.

EPIGRAM: A terse, witty poem.

EPITHALAMIUM: A wedding poem.

GEORGIC: A poem pertaining to agriculture.

HAIKU: Three unrhymed lines of five, seven, and five syllables.

LAY: A long narrative poem.

LIMERICK: A light verse of five lines with an AABBA rhyme scheme.

ODE: A formal lyric poem.

PASTORAL: An idealized depiction of rural life.

SONNET: A lyric poem of fourteen lines.

□ THE NINE MUSES

The Muses in Greek mythology are any of the nine daughters of Mnemosyne and Zeus, each of whom presided over a different art or science.

Calliope: *epic poetry*
Clio: *history*
Erato: *lyric poetry and mime*
Euterpe: *lyric poetry and music*
Melpomene: *tragedy*
Polyhymnia: *singing, rhetoric and mime*
Terpsichore: *dancing and choral singing*
Thalia: *comedy and pastoral poetry*
Urania: *astronomy*

□ SOME AUTHORS WITH MEDICAL DEGREES

Dannie Abse · Pio Barojo · Anton Chekhov · Peter Clement · Robin Cook · Patricia Cornwall · Michael Crichton · Jaime de Angulo · Alfred Döblin · Arthur Conan Doyle · Jonathan Gash · Tess Gerritsen · Oliver Wendell Holmes · Khaled Hosseini · Frank Huyler · Morio Kita · Perri Klass · Charles Lever · Carlo Levi · Vyvyane Loh · Somerset Maugham · Kita Morio · John Murray · Alan E. Nourse · Michael Palmer · M. Scott Peck · François Rabelais · Mickey Zucker Reichert · Jean-Christophe Rufin · Nawal El Saadawi · Frank Slaughter · Tobias Smollett · Saul Tchernichowsky · Dustin Thomason · Abraham Verghese · William Carlos Williams · F. Paul Wilson

☐ SOME BOOKISH IDIOMS

You can't tell a book by its cover
In his/her good books
Hit the books
Curl up with a good book
Crack a book
Bookworm
Every trick in the book
He/she wrote the book
Like an open book
Read him/her like a book
Read between the lines
Could fill a book
Read up on
Read you
Wax poetic
Poetic justice
Poetic license
Speaks volumes
That's one for the books
Chapter and verse
Easy read
Light reading
Heavy tome
Wide readership
Hot off the press
From cover to cover
Voracious reader
Bedside reading
Writer's block
Instant classic
Classic of its kind
Tell-all memoir
The common reader
Of a literary bent
Literary pretensions
Bodice-ripper
Page-turner

☐ SOME FULL NAMES

S(hmuel) Y(osef) Agnon · E(dward) M(organ) Forster
A(ntonia) S(usan) Byatt · J(ohn) M(ichael) Coetzee
E(dward) L(aurence) Doctorow · A(my) M. Homes
J(ames) P(atrick) Donleavy · C(live) S(taples) Lewis
E(dward) E(stlin) Cummings · T(homas) S(tearns) Eliot
J(ohn) R(onald) R(eul) Tolkien · W(ystan) H(ugh) Auden
J(erome) D(avid) Salinger · E(lwyn) B(rooks) White
V(idiadhar) S(urajprasad) Naipaul · P(hyllis) D(orothy) James
A(rchie) R(andolph) Ammons · J(ames) G(raham) Ballard
P(atrick) J(ake) O'Rourke · R(obert) L(awrence) Stine
P(elham) G(renville) Wodehouse · E(dith) J(oy) Scovell

☐ A FEW WRITERS WITH D.D.S. DEGREES

Zane Grey · Yu Hua · Faye Kellerman

□ SOME MOVIES ABOUT WRITERS

Hans Christian Andersen
Balzac: A Life of Passion
The Life of Emile Zola
The Bad Lord Byron
Devotion (the Brontë sisters)
Impromptu (George Sand)
Henry & June (Henry Miller)
Shakespeare in Love
Beloved Infidel (F. Scott Fitzgerald)
In Love and War (Hemingway)
Il Postino (Pablo Neruda)
Jack London
Sylvia (Sylvia Plath)
Iris (Iris Murdoch)
The Loves of Edgar Allan Poe
Shadowlands (C. S. Lewis)
Heartbeat (Jack Kerouac)
Wilde
Mrs. Parker and the Vicious Circle (Dorothy Parker)
Tom and Viv (T. S. Eliot)
Quills (Marquis de Sade)
The Hours (Virginia Woolf)
Finding Neverland (J. M. Barrie)
The Adventures of Mark Twain

□ OSCAR WINNERS BASED ON NOVELS

2003 *Lord of the Rings: Return of the King* (J. R. R. Tolkien)
1996 *The English Patient* (Michael Ondaatje)
1994 *Forrest Gump* (Winston Groom)
1993 *Schindler's List* (Thomas Keneally)
1991 *The Silence of the Lambs* (Thomas Harris)
1990 *Dances with Wolves* (Michael Blake)
1983 *Terms of Endearment* (Larry McMurtry)
1979 *Kramer vs. Kramer* (Avery Corman)
1980 *Ordinary People* (Judith Guest)
1975 *One Flew Over the Cuckoo's Nest* (Ken Kesey)

1974 *The Godfather II* (Mario Puzo)
1972 *The Godfather* (Mario Puzo)
1969 *Midnight Cowboy* (James Leo Herlihy)
1967 *In the Heat of the Night* (John Ball)
1963 *Tom Jones* (Henry Fielding)
1959 *Ben Hur* (Lew Wallace)
1958 *Gigi* (Colette)
1957 *The Bridge on the River Kwai* (Pierre Boulle)
1956 *Around the World in 80 Days* (Jules Verne)
1953 *From Here to Eternity* (James Jones)
1949 *All the King's Men* (Robert Penn Warren)
1947 *Gentleman's Agreement* (Laura Z. Hobson)
1946 *The Best Years of Our Lives* (Mackinlay Kantor)
1945 *The Lost Weekend* (Charles Jackson)
1942 *Mrs. Miniver* (Jan Struthers)
1941 *How Green Was My Valley* (Richard Llewellyn)
1940 *Rebecca* (Daphne Du Maurier)
1939 *Gone With the Wind* (Margaret Mitchell)
1935 *Mutiny on the Bounty* (Nordhoff & Hall)
1931 *Grand Hotel* (Vicki Baum)
1930 *Cimarron* (Edna Ferber)
1929 *All Quiet on the Western Front* (Erich Maria Remarque)

□ SOME DIRECTORS WHO HAVE WRITTEN FICTION

Woody Allen · Neil Jordan · Elia Kazan · Barry Levinson · Alan Parker · Oliver Stone · Melvin Van Peebles · Orson Welles

---

□ SOME SHORT STORIES MADE INTO FILMS

"Night Bus" (Samuel Hopkins Adams): *It Happened One Night*
"The Swimmer" (John Cheever): *The Swimmer*
"The Tin Star" (John W. Cunningham): *High Noon*
"Killings" (Andre Dubus): *In the Bedroom*
"Rear Window" (Cornell Woolrich): *Rear Window*
"Massacre" (James W. Bellah): *Fort Apache*
"The Killers" (Ernest Hemingway): *The Killers*

"The Man Who Would Be King" (Rudyard Kipling): *The Man Who Would Be King*
"The Wisdom of Eve" (Mary Orr): *All About Eve*
"Babette's Feast" (Isak Dinesen): *Babette's Feast*
"The Sentinel" (Arthur C. Clarke): *2001: A Space Odyssey*
"The Birds" (Daphne du Maurier): *The Birds*
"The Real Bad Friend" (Robert Bloch): *Psycho*
"Where Are You Going, Where Have You Been?" (Joyce Carol Oates): *Smooth Talk*
"The Palace Thief" (Ethan Canin): *The Emperor's Club*
"Supertoys Last All Summer Long" (Brian Wilson Aldiss): *A.I. Artifical Intelligence*
"The Age of Grief" (Jane Smiley): *The Secret Lives of Dentists*
"The Greatest Gift" (Philip van Doren Stern): *It's a Wonderful Life*
"Million Dollar Baby" (F. X. Toole): *Million Dollar Baby*

☐ SOME NOVEL-INTO-FILM TITLE CHANGES

The Brave Cowboy (Edward Abbey): *Lonely Are the Brave*
American Hero (Larry Beinhart): *Wag the Dog*
A Death in the Family (James Agee): *All the Way Home*
An American Tragedy (Theodore Dreiser): *A Place in the Sun*
The Hamlet (William Faulkner): *The Long Hot Summer*
Washington Square (Henry James): *The Heiress*
Horseman, Pass By (Larry McMurtry): *Hud*
Dog Soldiers (Robert Stone): *Who'll Stop the Rain*
Do Androids Dream of Electric Sheep? (Philip K. Dick): *Blade Runner*
Sometimes a Great Notion (Ken Kesey): *Never Give an Inch*
Pylon (William Faulkner): *The Tarnished Angels*
The Clansman (Thomas Dixon): *The Birth of a Nation*
Flowers for Algernon (Daniel Keyes): *Charley*
The Killer Angels (Michael Shaara): *Gettysburg*
Clean Break (Lionel White): *The Killing*
Down There (David Goodis): *Shoot the Piano Player*
Cutter and Bone (Newton Thornburg): *Cutter's Way*
Waltz into Darkness (Carnell Woolrich): *Original Sin*
The Blank Wall (Elizabeth Sanxay Holding): *The Deep End*

Jack's Return Home (Ted Lewis): *Get Carter*
Build My Gallows High (Geoffrey Homes): *Out of the Past*
Tainted Evidence (Robert Daley): *Night Falls on Manhattan*
Stray Dogs (John Ridley): *U-Turn*
Red Dragon (Thomas Harris): *Man Hunter*
Animal Husbandry (Laura Zigman): *Someone Like You*
Ripley's Game (Patricia Highsmith): *The American Friend*
The Talented Mr. Ripley (Patricia Highsmith): *Purple Noon*
Falling Angel (William Hjorstberg): *Angel Heart*
Our Sunshine (Robert Drewe): *Ned Kelly*
The Last Ride (Thomas Eidson): *Missing*
A Prayer for Owen Meany (John Irving): *Simon Birch*
Heartbreak Hotel (Anne Rivers Siddons): *Heart of Dixie*
A Widow for One Year (John Irving): *A Door in the Floor*
Vile Bodies (Evelyn Waugh): *Bright Young Things*
The Home Invaders (Frank Hohimer): *Thief*
Doll's Eyes (Bari Wood): *In Dreams*
The Club Dumas (Arturo Pérez-Reverte): *The Ninth Gate*
The Flanders Panel (Arturo Pérez-Reverte): *Uncovered*
58 Minutes (Walter Wager): *Die Hard 2*
Shoeless Joe (W. P. Kinsella): *Field of Dreams*
Theater (W. Somerset Maugham): *Being Julia*
Badge of Evil (Whit Masterson): *A Touch of Evil*
Tess of the d'Urbervilles (Thomas Hardy): *Tess*
Skipping Christmas (John Grisham): *Christmas with the Kranks*
The Mammy (Brendan O'Carroll): *Agnes Browne*
The Hunter (Donald Westlake): *Payback*
Bid Time Return (Richard Matheson): *Somewhere in Time*
Israel Rank (Roy Horniman): *Kind Hearts and Coronets*
Red Alert (Peter George): *Dr. Strangelove; or How I Learned to Stop Worrying and Love the Bomb…*
Monkey Planet (Pierre Boulle): *Planet of the Apes*

□ MOST SCREENPLAYS BASED ON AN AUTHOR'S WORK

There are 109 films based on the work of Western writer Zane Grey.

☐ SOME TV SERIES BASED ON NOVELS

All Creatures Great and Small: James Herriott,
All Creatures Great and Small
Dobie Gillis: Max Shulman, *The Affairs of Dobie Gillis*
Lassie: Eric Knight, *Lassie Come Home*
Little House on the Prairie: Laura Ingalls Wilder,
Little House on the Prairie
No Time For Sergeants: Mac Hyman, *No Time for Sergeants*
Peyton Place: Grace Metalious, *Peyton Place*
Sex and the City: Candace Bushnell, *Sex and the City*

☐ SOME OPERAS BASED ON NOVELS

An American Tragedy (Tobias Ricker): Theodore Dreiser,
An American Tragedy (1925)
Billy Budd (Benjamin Britten): Herman Melville,
Billy Budd (1926)
Carmen (Georges Bizet): Prosper Merimée, *Carmen* (1852)
Eugene Onegin (Pyotr Ilyich Tchaikovsky): Alexander Pushkin,
Eugene Onegin (1833)
La Bohème (Giacomo Puccini): Henri Murger, *Scènes de la vie de bohème* (1848)
Lakmé (Léo Delibes): Pierre Loti, *Le Mariage de Loti* (1880)
La Traviata (Giuseppe Verdi): Alexandre Dumas, *fils*,
La Dame aux caméllias (1852)
Lucia di Lammermoor (Gaetano Donizetti): Sir Walter Scott,
The Bride of Lammermoor (1819)
Manon (Jules Massenet): Abbé Prévost, *Manon Lescaut* (1731)
Porgy and Bess (George & Ira Gershwin): DuBose Heyward,
Porgy (1925)
Rienzi (Richard Wagner): Edward Bulwer-Lytton, *Rienzi, The Last of the Tribunes* (1835)
Rigoletto (Verdi): Victor Hugo, *Le Roi s'amuse* (1832)
Tales of Hoffman (Jacques Offenbach): E. T. A. Hoffman,
Weird Tales (1815)
Thaïs (Massenet): Anatole France, *Thaïs* (1890)
Werther (Massenet): Johann Wolfgang von Goethe,
The Sorrows of Young Werther (1774)

☐ SOME MUSICALS BASED ON FICTION

Cabaret (John Kander & Fred Ebb): Christopher Isherwood, *Berlin Stories*

Camelot (Alan Jay Lerner & Frederick Loewe): T. H. White, *The Once and Future King*

Cats (Andrew Lloyd Webber): T. S. Eliot, *Old Possum's Book of Practical Cats*

The Color Purple (Brenda Russell, Allee Willis, & Stephen Bray): Alice Walker, *The Color Purple*

Damn Yankees (Richard Adler & Jerry Ross): Douglas Wallop, *The Year the Yankees Lost the Pennant*

Fiddler on the Roof (Jerry Bock & Sheldon Harnick): Sholom Aleichem, *Tevye's Daughter*

Flower Drum Song (Richard Rodgers & Oscar Hammerstein II): C. Y. Lee, *Flower Drum Song*

Guys and Dolls (Frank Loesser): Damon Runyon, "The Idyll of Miss Sarah Brown"

Les Misérables (Alain Boublil & Claude-Michel Schönberg): Victor Hugo, *Les Misérables*

The Light in the Piazza (Adam Guettel): Elizabeth Spencer, *The Light in the Piazza*

Little Women (Jason Howland): Louisa May Alcott, *Little Women*

Lost in the Stars (Kurt Weill & Maxwell Anderson): Alan Paton, *Cry the Beloved Country*

Mame (Jerry Herman & Cy Coleman): Patrick Dennis, *Auntie Mame*

Man of La Mancha (Mitchell Leigh): Miguel Cervantes, *Don Quixote*

Oliver! (Lionel Bart): Charles Dickens, *Oliver Twist*

Pal Joey (Rodgers & Hammerstein): John O'Hara, *Pal Joey*

Ragtime (Stephen Flaherty & Lynn Ahrens): E. L. Doctorow, *Ragtime*

Show Boat (Jerome Kern & Oscar Hammerstein II): Edna Ferber, *Showboat*

South Pacific (Rodgers & Hammerstein): James Michener, *Tales of the South Pacific*

The Pajama Game (Adler & Ross): Richard Bissell, *7½¢*
The Phantom of the Opera (Andrew Lloyd Webber):
Gaston Leroux, *The Phantom of the Opera*
The Wiz (Charlie Smalls & William F. Brown): L. Frank Baum,
The Wonderful Wizard of Oz
Wonderful Town (Betty Comden & Adolph Green):
Ruth McKinney, *My Sister Eileen*

☐ TONY AWARD-WINNING DRAMAS ADAPTED FROM NOVELS

Desperate Hours · The Ballad of the Sad Café · The Grapes of Wrath · The Life and Adventures of Nicholas Nickleby · The Teahouse of the August Moon

---

☐ FIRST AMERICAN NOVEL TO BE ADAPTED TO THE STAGE

The Spy by James Fenimore Cooper premiered in 1821.

☐ THE ORIGINAL MODERN LIBRARY

The Modern Library of the World's Best Books first appeared in 1912 under the Boni & Liveright imprint. In 1925 it was purchased by Bennett Cerf, who founded the Modern Library Company. A few years later they decided to publish "random" works outside of the Modern Library guidelines and formed the Random House imprint. It became so successful that in a few more years it became the name of their enterprise and the Modern Library one of its imprints.

Poor People by Fedor Dostoeveski
The Red Lily by Anatole France
Plays by Henrik Ibsen
Soldiers Three by Rudyard Kipling
Plays by Maurice Maeterlinck
Thus Spake Zarathustra by Friedrich Nietzsche
Studies in Pessimism by Arthur Schopenhauer
Treasure Island by Robert Louis Stevenson

Married by August Strindberg
The War in the Air by H. G. Wells
Plays by Oscar Wilde
The Picture of Dorian Gray by Oscar Wilde

□ THE FIRST DIME NOVEL

Malaeska, the Indian Wife of the White Hunter by Ann S. Stephens was the first dime novel. Printed in 1859 by Irwin P. Beadle and Company as its first title in the Beadle's Dime Novels series, it sold about 200,000 copies during the first year of publication.

□ FIRST PAPERBACK BOOKSHOP

The first bookshop to sell paperbacks exclusively was the City Lights Book Shop, established by the poet Lawrence Ferlinghetti in San Francisco's North Beach in 1953.

□ FIRST POCKET BOOKS

New York publisher Robert de Graff brought out the 25¢ Pocket Books with the kangaroo logo in 1939. The first ten titles were:

1. *Lost Horizon* by James Hilton
2. *Wake Up and Live!* By Dorothea Brande
3. *Five Great Tragedies* by William Shakespeare
4. *Topper* by Thorne Smith
5. *The Murder of Roger Ackroyd* by Agatha Christie
6. *Enough Rope* by Dorothy Parker
7. *Wuthering Heights* by Emily Brontë
8. *The Way of All Flesh* by Samuel Butler
9. *The Bridge of San Luis Rey* by Thornton Wilder
10. *Bambi* by Felix Salten

□ FIRST PAPERBACK MILLION SELLER

Dale Carnegie's self-help classic, *How to Win Friends and Influence People,* was Pocket Books' first million seller.

☐ FIRST PENGUIN PAPERBACKS (JULY 1935)

A Farewell to Arms by Ernest Hemingway
Madame Claire by Susan Ertz
Carnival by Compton Mackenzie
Ariel by André Maurois
Murder in the Vicarage by Agatha Christie
Poets' Pub by Eric Linklater
Twenty-Five by Beverly Nichols
William by E. H. Young
Gone to Earth by Mary Webb
The Unpleasantness at the Bellona Club by Dorothy L. Sayers

☐ SOME REALLY BIG NOVELS IN ENGLISH

The longest novel in English is Anthony Powell's twelve-volume *A Dance to the Music of Time* (1951–75). Among the longest modern single-volume novels are *Hunger's Brides* (2005) by Paul Anderson (1376 pp.) and *A Suitable Boy* (1993) by Vikram Seth (1400 pp.)

☐ TEN BEST TWENTIETH-CENTURY NOVELS IN ENGLISH

In 1996 Random House's Modern Library imprint issued its controversial list of the best novels in English published during the twentieth century. Here are the first ten:

1. *Ulysses* by James Joyce
2. *The Great Gatsby* by F. Scott Fitzgerald
3. *A Portrait of the Artist as a Young Man* by James Joyce
4. *Lolita* by Vladimir Nabokov
5. *Brave New World* by Aldous Huxley
6. *The Sound and the Fury* by William Faulkner
7. *Catch-22* by Joseph Heller
8. *Darkness at Noon* by Arthur Koestler
9. *Sons and Lovers* by D. H. Lawrence
10. *The Grapes of Wrath* by John Steinbeck

☐ BEST LESBIAN AND GAY NOVELS

Here are the top ten of the one hundred best gay and lesbian titles compiled by the Publishing Triangle, the association of lesbians and gay men in publishing:

Death in Venice by Thomas Mann
Giovanni's Room by James Baldwin
Our Lady of the Flowers by Jean Genet
Remembrance of Things Past by Marcel Proust
The Immoralist by André Gide
Orlando by Virginia Woolf
The Well of Loneliness by Radclyffe Hall
Kiss of the Spider Woman by Manuel Puig
The Memoirs of Hadrian by Marguerite Yourcenar
Zami by Audre Lord

☐ SOME ROTTEN REVIEWS

Of Mice and Men (Steinbeck): An oxymoronic combination of the tough and tender, *Of Mice and Men* will appeal to sentimental cynics, cynical sentimentalists.... Readers less easily thrown off their trolley will still prefer Hans Andersen. – *Time*

The Great Gatsby (Fitzgerald): What has never been alive cannot very well go on living. So this is a book of the season only.
– *New York Herald Tribune*

The Moviegoer (Percy): Mr. Percy's prose needs oil and a good checkup. – *The New Yorker*

For Whom the Bell Tolls (Hemingway): This book offers not pleasure but mounting pain; as literature it lacks the reserve that steadies genius and that lack not only dims its brilliance but makes it dangerous in its influence. – *Catholic World*

Under the Volcano (Lowry): Mr. Lowry is passionately in earnest about what he had to say concerning human hope and defeat, but for all his earnestness he has succeeded only in writing a rather good imitation of an important novel.
– *The New Yorker*

Miss Lonelyhearts (West): A knowledge of its contents will be essential to conversational poise in contemporary literature during the next three months – perhaps.

– *Boston Evening Telegraph*

Catch-22 (Heller): It gasps for want of craft and sensibility.... The book is an emotional hodgepodge; no mood is sustained long enough to register for more than a chapter.

– *New York Times Book Review*

☐ THE SEVEN COMMANDMENTS OF ANIMAL FARM

1. Whatever goes upon two legs is an enemy.
2. Whatever goes upon four legs, or has wings, is a friend.
3. No animal shall wear clothes.
4. No animal shall sleep in a bed.
5. No animal shall drink alcohol.
6. No animal shall kill any other animal.
7. All animals are equal.

☐ HUNGRY MIND'S BEST BOOKS

The Hungry Mind Review *published its list of the one hundred best books of the twentieth century. The first ten are:*

1. *The Education of Henry Adams* by Henry Adams
2. *Let Us Now Praise Famous Men* by James Agee and Walker Evans
3. *Bastard Out of Carolina* by Dorothy Allison
4. *Bless Me Ultima* by Rudolfo Anaya
5. *Winesburg, Ohio* by Sherwood Anderson
6. *I Know Why the Caged Bird Sings* by Maya Angelou
7. *Borderlands/La Frontera: The New Mestiza* by Gloria Anzaldúa
8. *Go Tell It on the Mountain* by James Baldwin
9. *The Price of the Ticket: Collected Nonfiction* by James Baldwin
10. *Slaves in the Family* by Edward Ball

☐ TEN MOST INFLUENTIAL TWENTIETH-CENTURY NOVELS

In 1998 Library Journal *published a list of 150 twentieth-century fiction titles regarded by librarians as the most influential either in the larger world or in their impact on them personally.*

1. *To Kill a Mockingbird* by Harper Lee
2. *Catcher in the Rye* by J. D. Salinger
3. *Lord of the Rings* by J. R. R. Tolkien
4. *Gone With the Wind* by Margaret Mitchell
5. *Beloved* by Toni Morrison
6. *The Color Purple* by Alice Walker
7. *1984* by George Orwell
8. *Animal Farm* by George Orwell
9. *Lord of the Flies* by William Golding
10. *Catch-22* by Joseph Heller

☐ HARPER BROTHERS

James and John Harper began their company in New York in 1818 with John Locke's *An Essay Concerning Human Understanding*. Early authors included Dickens, Thackeray, George Eliot, William Dean Howells, Thomas Hardy, Theodore Dreiser.

☐ BOOKS OF OPTIMISM, JOY, & GENTILITY

The New York Public Library's "Books of the [Twentieth] Century" included this category:

Elizabeth Bishop, *The Complete Poems*
Margaret Wise Brown, *Goodnight Moon*
Willa Cather, *Shadows on the Rock*
G. K. Chesterton, *The Innocence of Father Brown*
Langston Hughes, *The Best of Simple*
Sarah Orne Jewett, *The Country of the Pointed Firs*
Juan Ramón Jiménez, *Platero and I: An Andalusian Elegy*
Helen Keller, *The Story of My Life*
Harper Lee, *To Kill a Mockingbird*

A. A. Milne, *Winnie-the-Pooh*
Emily Post, *Etiquette in Society, in Business, in Politics, and at Home*
Irma S. Rombauer, *The Joy of Cooking*
George Bernard Shaw, *Pygmalion*
J. R. R. Tolkien, *The Hobbit*
P. G. Wodehouse, *The Inimitable Jeeves*

□ DISCOVER GREAT NEW WRITERS

Barnes & Noble introduced the Discover Great New Writers Award in 1993 to celebrate the work of first-time authors. Fiction winners are:

2004: *Heaven Lake* by John Dalton
2003: *Brick Lane* by Monica Ali
2002: *The Shell Collector* by Anthony Doerr
2001: *The Death of Vishnu* by Manil Suri
2000: *Girl with a Pearl Earring* by Tracy Chevalier
1999: *The Pleasing Hour* by Lily King
1998: *Rose's Garden* by Carrie Brown
1997: *The Light of Falling Stars* by J. Robert Lennon
1996: *The Giant's House* by Elizabeth McCracken
1995: *Native Speaker* by Chang-rae Lee
1994: *Snow Falling on Cedars* by David Guterson
1993: *A Place Where the Sea Remembers* by Sandra Benitez

□ DISTINGUISHED CONTRIBUTORS

The National Book Foundation (est 1988) presents a Medal for Distinguished Contribution to American Letters to a person who has "enriched our literary heritage over a life of service, or a corpus of work."

Judy Blume · Ray Bradbury · Gwendolyn Brooks · Clifton Fadiman · Stephen King · James Laughlin · David McCullough · Arthur Miller · Toni Morrison · Philip Roth · Studs Terkel · John Updike · Eudora Welty · Oprah Winfrey

◻ AUTHORS ON U.S. STAMPS

Louisa May Alcott · James Baldwin · Frank L. Baum · Stephen Vincent Benét · Pearl S. Buck · Willa Cather · James Fenimore Cooper · Emily Dickinson · T. S. Eliot · Ralph Waldo Emerson · Nathaniel Hawthorne · Ernest Hemingway · Langston Hughes · Zora Neale Hurston · Washington Irving · Robinson Jeffers · James Weldon Johnson · Sidney Lanier · Jack London · Henry Wadsworth Longfellow · Herman Melville · Edna St. Vincent Millay · Margaret Mitchell · Marianne Moore · Eugene O'Neill · Dorothy Parker · Edgar Allan Poe · Ayn Rand · Carl Sandburg · William Saroyan · Dr. Seuss · John Steinbeck · Henry David Thoreau · James Thurber · Mark Twain · Edith Wharton · Robert Penn Warren · John Greenleaf Whittier · Laura Ingalls Wilder · Tennessee Williams · Thomas Wolfe

---

◻ SOME EDITH WHARTON SIMILES

Literature's like a big railway station ... there's a train starting every minute.

The chairs and tables looked like poor relations who had repaid their keep by a long career of grudging usefulness.

Success on some men looks like a borrowed coat; it sits on you as though it had been made to order.

Hedges as solid as walls.

[Moving from a slow to a fast-paced life] was like stepping from a gondola to an ocean steamer.

Wisps of hair, like sunburst grass hanging over eyes as clear as pale grey crystals.

She reminded him, in her limp dust-colored garments, of last year's moth shaken out of the curtains of an empty house.

He stood before them, like a prisoner at the bar, or rather like a sick man before the physicians who were to heal him.

My words slipped from me like broken weapons.

EDITH WHARTON

His brain was like a brightly lit factory, full of flying wheels and precision.

A flash of pain darted through her, like the ripple of sheet lightning.

Mouth as sweet as a ripe fig.

Her vivid smile was like a light held up to dazzle me.

Temptation leapt on him like the stab of a knife.

Lifeless sky . . . like the first day of creation.

The lawn looked as expansive as a velvet carpet woven in one piece.

Looking calm as an eggshell.

The soundness of his nature was like the pure paste under a fine glaze.

Eyes peering between folds of fat like almond kernels in half-split shells.

☐ U.S. NOBEL PRIZE WINNERS (LITERATURE)

Saul Bellow · Joseph Brodsky · Pearl S. Buck · William Faulkner · Ernest Hemingway · Sinclair Lewis · Czelaw Milosz · Toni Morrison · Eugene O'Neill · Isaac Bashevis Singer · John Steinbeck

---

☐ MULTIPLE WINNERS OF THE PULITZER PRIZE (FICTION)

John Cheever (2) · William Faulkner (2)
Booth Tarkington (2) · John Updike (3)

☐ SOME IVY LEAGUE WRITERS

Brown

Donald Antrim · Peter Balakian · Barry Beckham · Sarah Shun-Lien Bynum · Susan Cheever · Tom Drury · Jeffrey Eugenides ·

Percival L. Everett · Richard Foreman · Andrew Sean Greer · John Hay · Tony Horwitz · E. Howard Hunt · Gayl Jones · Richard Kostelanetz · Mark McGarrity · Hilary Masters · Steven Millhauser · Susan Minot · Rick Moody · S. J. Perelman · Marilynne Robinson · Joanna Scott · Winfield Townley Scott · Jim Shepard · David Shields · Alison Smith · Marian Thurm · Alfred Uhry · Sherley Anne Williams

Columbia

Edward Albee · Isaac Asimov · Paul Auster · John Berryman · Robert Bingham · Bennet Cerf · Laurie Colwin · Alfred Corn · Beverly Donofrio · Jason Epstein · Allen Ginsberg · John Hollander · Richard Howard · Langston Hughes · Alfred Kazin · Jack Kerouac · Alfred Knopf · Kenneth Koch · Joseph Wood Krutch · Tony Kushner · Audre Lord · Thomas Merton · Terrence McNally · Robert Silverberg · Louis Simpson · Lionel Trilling · Dan Wakefield · Herman Wouk

Cornell

Diane Ackerman · A. Manette Ansay · Morris Bishop · Chana Bloch · Harold Bloom · Louis Bromfield · Susan Brownmiller · Pearl S. Buck · Susan Choi · Junot Díaz · Edward Jay Epstein · Richard Fariña · William H. Gass · Philip Gourevitch · Doris Grumbach · Laura Z. Hobson · Laura Riding Jackson · Judith Kelman · Arthur Laurents · Lorrie Moore · Toni Morrison · Manuel Muñoz · Stewart O'Nan · George Jean Nathan · Julie Orringer · Thomas Perry · Richard Price · Thomas Pynchon · Nina Revoyr · Kenneth Roberts · Matt Ruff · William T. Vollmann · Kurt Vonnegut, Jr. · Lauren Weisberger · E. B. White · Alice Dunbar-Wilson

Dartmouth

Carlos Baker · Philip Booth · William Bronk · Joseph Campbell · Evan S. Connell · Dinesh D'Souza · Richard Eberhardt · Louise Erdrich · Robert Frost · Theodore (Dr. Seuss) Geisel · Frank D. Gilroy · David R. Godine · William Hjortsberg · Richard Hovey · A. J. Liebling · Robert Pack · Gregory Rabassa · Budd Schulberg · Paula Sharp · Roger Simon · Lawrence Treat

HARVARD

Henry Adams · James Agee · Conrad Aiken · Horatio Alger, Jr. · Earl Derr Biggers · Robert Bly · Harold Brodkey · Judy Budnitz · John Horne Burns · Witter Bynner · Max Byrd · Bliss Carman · William Ellery Channing · John Jay Chapman · James Gould Cozzens · Countee Cullen · E. E. Cummings · Richard Henry Dana, Jr. · John Dos Passos · W. E. B. Du Bois · Christopher Durang · T. S. Eliot · Dudley Fitts · Ian Frazier · Nell Freudenberger · William Gaddis · Gish Jen · Thomas Gifford · Arthur Golden · Allegra Goodman · Donald Hall · Mark Helprin · Edward Hoagland · Adam Hochschild · John Hollander · Oliver Wendell Holmes · Pico Iyer · William James · Joseph Kanon · Tracy Kidder · Stanley Kunitz · Oliver LaFarge · Gregory McDonald · Archibald MacLeish · Norman Mailer · John P. Marquand · Francis Parkman · George Plimpton · Mary Rakow · John Reed · Edwin Arlington Robinson · Roger Rosenblatt · Meg Rosoff · L. E. Sissman · Logan Pearsall Smith · W. M. Spackman · Edward Taylor · Dustin Thomason · Henry David Thoreau · Peter Viereck · Theodore H. White · Colson Whitehead · Richard Wilbur · Sloan Wilson · Owen Wister · Thomas Wolfe

PENN

Charles Addams · Daniel Akst · Walter Annenberg · A. A. Attanasio · Alfred Bester · David Bradley · Olga Broumas · Noam Chomsky · Jennifer Egan · Loren Eisley · Robert Elegant · Stanley Fish · Nikki Giovanni · Zane Grey · Alan Gurganus · Edward Hirsch · Kristin Hunter · Caroline Hwang · Joe Klein · Erik Larson · Eve Merriam · Chaim Potok · Ezra Pound · Lisa Scottoline · Susan Richards · Anita Shreve · Martin Cruz Smith · John Edgar Wideman · C. K. Williams · William Carlos Williams

PRINCETON

Madison Smartt Bell · Pinckney Benedict · A. Scott Berg · John Peale Bishop · Chris Bohjalian · H. H. Brackenridge · Ian Caldwell · Robert A. Caro · Robert P. Tristram Coffin · Frank Deford · José Donoso · John Gregory Dunne · Jonathan Safran Foer · F. Scott Fitzgerald · Philip Freneau · George Garrett · Jane Hirschfield ·

Galway Kinnell · Walter Kirn · Alan Lightman · Harry Mathews · T. S. Matthews · John McPhee · William Meredith · W. S. Merwin · Darcy O'Brien · Tom Paine · Jodi Picoult · David Remnick · Booth Tarkington · Thornton Wilder · Edmund Wilson

YALE

Peter Ackroyd · Philip Barry · Stephen Vincent Benét · Susan Brownrigg · Lan Samantha Chang · Frederick Crews · Clarence Day · Michael Dorris · Brendan Gill · Zoë Heller · John Hersey · Yolanda Joe · Michiko Kakutani · John Knowles · David Leavitt · Max Lerner · Sinclair Lewis · Aimee E. Liu · Dwight Macdonald · Archibald MacLeish · David McCullough · Paul Monette · Gloria Naylor · Ann Packer · Z. Z. Packer · Christina Schwarz · Donald Ogden Stewart · Mark Strand · Calvin Trillin · Noah Webster · James Wilcox · Thornton Wilder · Tom Wolfe

---

☐ BELLWETHER PRIZE: BOOKS IN SUPPORT OF SOCIAL CHANGE

In 2000 Barbara Kingsolver founded and funded the Bellwether Prize of $25,000 to be awarded in even-numbered years to an unpublished manuscript by a writer who has not yet published a book. It is the only major North American prize for the arts that specifically seeks to support a literature of social responsibility.

2004 Marjorie Kowalski Cole, *Correcting the Landscape*
2002 Gayle Brandeis, *The Book of Dead Birds*
2000 Donna M. Gershten, *Kissing the Virgin's Mouth*

☐ SOME AMERICAN WRITERS WHO DIED IN THEIR THIRTIES

Charles Brockden Brown (39) · John Horne Burns (37) · Iris Chang (36) · Hart Crane (33) · Amanda Davis (32) · Paul Laurence Dunbar (34) · Jacques Futrelle (37) · Donald Goines (36) · Lucy Grealy (39) · Lorraine Hansberry (35) · Thomas Heggen (30) · Joyce Kilmer (32) · Cyril M. Kornbluth (34) · Sidney Lanier (39) · Emma Lazarus (38) · Larry Levis (39) · Ross Lockridge (34) · Grace Metalious (39) · Frank Norris (32)

Flannery O'Connor (39) · Sylvia Plath (31) · John Reed (33) · Trumbull Stickney (30) · Edward Lewis Wallant (36) · Artemus Ward (33) · Nathanael West (37) · Phillis Wheatley (31) · Thomas Wolfe (38)

□ SOME YOUNG LIONS

Since 2001 the New York Public Library has presented its Young Lions Fiction Award to an American author under the age of thirty-five who has published a work of fiction during the year.

2005 Andrew Sean Green, *The Confessions of Max Tivoli*
2004 Monique Truong, *The Book of Salt*
2003 Anthony Doerr, *The Shell Collector*
2002 Colson Whitehead, *John Henry Days*
2001 Mark Z. Danielewski, *House of Leaves*

□ BOOKS THAT SHAPED THE AMERICAN CHARACTER

In 1985 American Heritage *magazine asked Jonathan Yardley to write an article to be called "Ten Books That Shaped the American Character." His selections:*

1. *Walden* by Henry David Thoreau (1854)
2. *Leaves of Grass* by Walt Whitman (1855)
3. *Ragged Dick, or Street Life in New York* by Horatio Alger (1867)
4. *The Adventures of Huckleberry Finn* by Mark Twain (1884)
5. *The Boston Cooking School Cookbook* by Fannie Farmer (1896)
6. *The Theory of the Leisure Class* by Thorstein Veblen (1899)
7. *The Souls of Black Folk* by W. E. B. Du Bois (1903)
8. *In Our Time* by Ernest Hemingway (1925)
9. *How to Win Friends and Influence People* by Dale Carnegie (1936)
10. *The Common Sense Book of Baby and Child Care* by Benjamin Spock, M.D. (1946)

☐ FIRST WRITERS' CONFERENCE IN AMERICA

Bread Loaf Writers' Conference, established 1926.

☐ SOME IOWA WRITERS' WORKSHOP GRADUATES

The Iowa Writers' Workshop at the University of Iowa was the first creative writing degree program in a U. S. university.

Marvin Bell · T. C. Boyle · Ethan Canin · Raymond Carver · R. V. Cassill · Lan Samantha Chang · Sandra Cisneros · Michael Cunningham · Charles D'Ambrosio · Andre Dubus · Nathan Englander · Jorie Graham · Jennifer Haigh · Joy Harjo · Colin Harrison · A. M. Homes · John Irving · Thom Jones · W. P. Kinsella · Sena Jeter Naslund · Flannery O'Connor · Chris Offut · Z. Z. Packer · Ann Padgett · Jayne Anne Phillips · Jane Smiley · Wallace Stegner · Anthony Swofford · John Edgar Wideman · Joy Williams

---

☐ SOME AMERICAN PSEUDONYMS

Ai (Florence Anthony)
Max Brand (Frederick Faust)
Jennifer Crusie (Jennifer Smith)
Patrick Dennis (Edward E. Tanner III)
Jude Deveraux (Jude Gilliam White)
Ellen Douglas (Josephine Haxton)
Nicholas Gage (Nikos Gatzoyiannis)
O. Henry (William Sidney Porter)
Andrew Holleran (Eric Garber)
Ha Jin (Xuefi Jin)
Ed McBain (Evan Hunter)
Fern Michaels (Mary Kuzkir)
Amanda Quick (Jayne Ann Krentz)
Ayn Rand (Alissa Rosenbaum)
J. D. Robb (Nora Roberts)
Luke Short (Frederick Glidden)

Meryle Secrest (June Doman)
Dr. Seuss (Theodore Seuss Geisel)
Mark Twain (Samuel Clemens)
Ed Vega (Edgardo Verga Yunque)
Nathanael West (Nathan Weinstein)
Tennessee Williams (Thomas Lanier Williams)

☐ MULTIPLE PULITZER PRIZE WINNERS

Norman Mailer, once for a novel and once for nonfiction; Robert Penn Warren, once for a novel and twice for poetry; and Thornton Wilder, once for a novel and twice for drama.

☐ THEY ATTENDED KENYON COLLEGE

Caleb Carr · Tracy Chevalier · Carl Djerassi · E. L. Doctorow · Daniel Mark Epstein · William H. Gass · Anthony Hecht · Robert Lowell · Robie Macauley · Robert Mezey · Peter Taylor · James Wright

---

☐ WISDOM OF MARK TWAIN

Clothes make the man. Naked people have little or no influence on society.

Don't go around saying the world owes you a living. The world owes you nothing. It was here first.

Fiction is obliged to stick to possibilities. Truth isn't.

I didn't attend the funeral, but I sent a nice letter saying that I approved of it.

In the first place, God made idiots. That was for practice. Then he made school boards.

It is better to keep your mouth closed and let people think you are a fool than to open it and remove all doubt.

It usually takes more than three weeks to prepare a good impromptu speech.

Familiarity breeds contempt – and children.

Never put off until tomorrow what you can do the day after tomorrow.

Let us so live that when we come to die even the undertaker will be sorry.

You cannot depend on your eyes when your imagination is out of focus.

Water, taken in moderation, cannot hurt anybody.

Man is the only animal that blushes. Or needs to.

All you need in life is ignorance and confidence; then success is sure.

Few things are harder to put up with than the annoyance of a good example.

A classic is something that everybody wants to have read and nobody wants to read.

A banker is a fellow who lends you an umbrella when the sun is shining, but wants it back the minute it begins to rain.

Always acknowledge a fault. This will throw those in authority off their guard and give you an opportunity to commit more.

I never let my schooling interfere with my education.

Beware of reading health books. You may die of a misprint.

□ AMERICAN AUTHORS PRONUNCIATION GUIDE

Edward Albee: ALL-bee
Isabel Allende: ah-YEN-day
Maya Angelou: AHN-ge-low
Louis Auchincloss: AW-kin-claws
Jean M. Auel: OWL
Donald Barthelme: BAR-thelm
T. Coraghessan Boyle: kuh-RAG-issun
Dan Chaon: SHAWN

Michael Chrichton: CRY-ton
Edwige Danticat: Ed-WEEDJ Dan-ti-CAH
Junot Díaz: HOO-note DEE-ahss
W. E. B. Du Bois: du BOYCE
Andre Dubus: duh-BYOOS
Pam Durban: Dur-BAN
Paul Fussell: rhymes with "Russell"
Diana Gabaldon: GAB-ahl-dohn
Dana Gioia: JOY-ah
Louise Glück: GLICK
Chaim Grade: GRA-duh
Shirley Ann Grau: GROW
Dashiell Hammett: duh-SHEEL HAM-uht
Kent Haruf: like "sheriff"
Oscar Hijuelos: ee-WAY-los
Khaled Hossein: HAH-led ho-SEE-nee
David Henry Hwang: WONG
Randall Jarrell: juh-REL
Ursula K. Le Guin: luh-GWIN
Madeleine L'Engle: Lang-EL
John Lescroart: LES-qua
Don Marquis: MAR-kwis
Peter Matthiessen: MATH-eh-son
Czelaw Milosz: MEE-wosh
Vladimir Nabokov: Vla-DEE-meer Nah-BOAK-off
Chuck Palahnuik: pau-LA-nick
W. Annie Proulx: PROO
Theodore Roethke: RET-kee
Edward Said: Sa-EED
Luc Sante: Luke SAHNT
Lisa Scottoline: Skoh-toe-LEEN-ee
Ntozake Shange: En-TO-za-ki SHONG-yay
Tad Szulc: SHULZ
Paul Theroux: Thuh-ROO
Henry Thoreau: THOR-oh
Andrew Vachs: VAX
Joseph Wambaugh: WAHM-bow

☐ MOST PROLIFIC AMERICAN AUTHOR

Lauran Paine (1916–1995) wrote more than nine hundred books, principally westerns, romance novels, and mysteries, under an assortment of pen names.

☐ FIRST NOVEL PUBLISHED IN THE UNITED STATES

The Power of Sympathy (1789) by William Hill Brown

☐ SOME "SEVEN SISTERS" SISTERS

BARNARD

Laurie Anderson · Natalie Angier · Mary Antin · Charlotte Armstrong · Nora Balakian · Elizabeth Benedict · Anne Bernays · Mei-Mei Berssenbrugge · Rosellen Brown · Janet Burroway · Hortense Calisher · Arlene Croce · Edwige Danticat · Lydia Davis · Thulani Davis · Stacey D'Erasmo · Babette Deutsch · Cristina Garcia · Rebecca Goldstein · Mary Gordon · Francine du Plessix Gray · Patricia Highsmith · Anne Hollander · Jean Houston · Zora Neale Hurston · Elizabeth Janeway · Tama Janowitz · Joyce Johnson · June Jordan · Jhumpa Lahiri · Margaret Mead · Daphne Merkin · Eliza Minot · Alice Notley · Sigrid Nunez · Belva Plain · Emily Prager · Anna Quindlen · Cathleen Schine · Ntozake Shange · Martha Stewart · Ellen Willis

BRYN MAWR

Renata Adler · A. S. Byatt · Elizabeth Daly · Hilda Doolittle · Martha Gellhorn · Edith Hamilton · Marianne Moore · Sabina Murray · Lynn Sharon Schwartz · Elaine Showalter · Kathryn S. White

MOUNT HOLYOKE

Virginia Adair · Lynne Barrett · Carol Higgins Clark · Emily Dickinson · Susan-Lori Parks · Gjertrud Schnackenberg · Wendy Wasserstein

Radcliffe

Alice Adams · Ann Arensberg · Margaret Atwood · Sallie Bingham · Ann Cameron · Jay Cantor · Susan Conant · Barbara Epstein · Rachel Field · Louise Glück · Allegra Goodman · Ellen Goodman · Beth Gutcheon · Julie Hayden · Suzanne K. Langer · Andrea Lee · Ursula K. Le Guin · Alison Lurie · Anne McCaffrey · Heather McHugh · Emily Mann · Sue Miller · Jane O'Reilly · Linda Pastan · Katha Pollitt · Francine Prose · Adrienne Rich · Phyllis Rose · Gertrude Stein · Jean Strouse · Diana Trilling · Barbara Tuchman · Jean Valentine

Smith

Natalie Babbitt · Julia Child · Barbara Cooney · Maureen Howard · Barbara Leaming · Anne Morrow Lindbergh · Margaret Mitchell · Ruth Ozeki · Sylvia Plath · Cynthia Voight · Jane Yolen

Vassar

Shana Alexander · Elizabeth Bishop · Elizabeth Coatsworth · Linda Fairstein · Jane Kramer · Mary McCarthy · Edna St. Vincent Millay · Ellen Moers

Wellesley

Lisa Alther · Carol Bly · Sally Carrighar · Marjory Stoneman Douglas · Nora Ephron · Hannah Green · Carolyn J. Heilbrun · Judith Krantz · Judith Martin · Judith Mitchell · Linda Nochlin · Mary Oliver · Santha Rama Rau · Muriel Rukeyser · Jane Smiley · Reetika Vazirani · Ann Zwinger

---

□ BEST BOOKS OF AMERICAN HISTORY OF THE LAST QUARTER CENTURY

These books have won the Pulitzer Prize for history:

2005 *Washington's Crossing* by David Hackett Fisher
2004 *A Nation Under Our Feet: Black Political Struggles in the Rural South from Slavery to the Great Migration* by Steven Hahn
2003 *An Army at Dawn: The War in North Africa, 1942–1943* by Rick Atkinson

2002 *The Metaphysical Club: A Story of Ideas in America* by Louis Menand
2001 *Founding Brothers: The Revolutionary Generation* by Joseph J. Ellis
2000 *Freedom From Fear: The American People in Depression and War, 1929–1945* by David M. Kennedy
1999 *Gotham: A History of New York City to 1898* by Edwin G. Burrows and Mike Wallace
1998 *Summer for the Gods: The Scopes Trial and America's Continuing Debate over Science and Religion* by Edward J. Larson
1997 *Original Meanings: Politics and Ideas in the Making of the Constitution* by Jack N. Rakove
1996 *William Cooper's Town: Power and Persuasion on the Frontier of the Early American Republic* by Alan Taylor
1995 *No Ordinary Time: Franklin and Eleanor Roosevelt: The Home Front in World War II* by Doris Kearns Goodwin
1994 No Award
1993 *The Radicalism of the American Revolution* by Gordon S. Wood
1992 *The Fate of Liberty: Abraham Lincoln and Civil Liberties* by Mark E. Neely, Jr.
1991 *A Midwife's Tale* by Laurel Thatcher Ulrich
1990 *In Our Image: America's Empire in the Philippines* by Stanley Karnow
1989 *Parting the Waters: America in the King Years 1954–1963* by Taylor Branch
1989 *Battle Cry of Freedom: The Civil War Era* by James M. McPherson
1988 *The Launching of Modern American Science 1846–1876* by Robert V. Bruce
1987 *Voyagers to the West: A Passage in the Peopling of America on the Eve of the Revolution* by Bernard Bailyn
1986 *. . . the Heavens and the Earth: A Political History of the Space Age* by Walter A. McDougall
1985 *Prophets of Regulation* by Thomas K. McCraw
1984 No Award

1983 *The Transformation of Virginia, 1740–1790* by Rhys L. Isaac
1982 *Mary Chesnut's Civil War* edited by C. Vann Woodward
1981 *American Education: The National Experience, 1783–1876* by Lawrence A. Cremin
1980 *Been in the Storm So Long* by Leon F. Litwack

□ "GENIUS AWARD" NOVELISTS

These fiction writers have been named MacArthur Fellows since the inception of the program in 1981:

Walter Abish
Andrea Barrett
Octavia Butler
Jay Cantor
Sandra Cisneros
Guy Davenport
Lydia Davis
Andre Dubus
William Gaddis
Ernest J. Gaines
Rebecca Goldstein
Virginia Hamilton
Patricia Hampl
Aleksandar Hemon
Karen Hesse
Bette Howland
Ruth Prawer Jhabvala
Charles Johnson
Edward P. Jones
William Kennedy
Norman Manea
Paule Marshall
Cormac McCarthy
James MacPherson
Ved Mehta
Richard Powers
Thomas Pynchon
Ishmael Reed
Joanna Scott
Leslie Marmon Silko
David Foster Wallace
Colson Whitehead
John Edgar Wideman

□ SOME CHARACTER NAMES FROM THOMAS PYNCHON NOVELS

Benny Profane · Mucho Maas · Zoyd Wheeler
Tyrone Slothrop · McClintic Sphere · Laszlo Jamf · Teddy Bloat
Grover Snodd · Tantivy Mucker-Maffick · Clayton Chiclitz
Stanley Koteks · Mike Fallopian

☐ SUMMARY OF THE LESSONS OF HISTORY IN FOUR SENTENCES

1. Whom the gods would destroy, they first make mad with power.
2. The mills of God grind slowly, but they grind exceeding small.
3. The bee fertilizes the flower it robs.
4. When it is dark enough, you can see the stars.

– from *The Practical Cogitator* by Charles A. Beard

☐ SOME NEW DIRECTIONS WRITERS

James Laughlin (1914–97), the founder and for sixty years the publisher of New Directions, was the premier independent publisher of his era. He brought out books by some of the most revolutionary writers of his time, including:

Djuana Barnes · John Hawkes · Henry Miller · Yukio Mishima Vladimir Nabokov · Octavio Paz · Ezra Pound · Delmore Schwartz · Muriel Spark · Dylan Thomas · Nathanael West · Tennessee Williams · William Carlos Williams

---

☐ OPRAH'S BOOK CLUB SELECTIONS

2005 William Faulkner, *As I Lay Dying, The Sound and the Fury*, and *Light in August*
2004 Gabriel García Márquez, *One Hundred Years of Solitude*
Carson McCullers, *The Heart Is a Lonely Hunter*
Leo Tolstoy, *Anna Karenina*
Pearl S. Buck, *The Good Earth*
2003 John Steinbeck, *East of Eden*
Alan Paton, *Cry, the Beloved Country*
2002 Ann-Marie MacDonald, *Fall on Your Knees*
Toni Morrison, *Sula*
2001 Jonathan Franzen, *The Corrections*
Rohinton Mistry, *A Fine Balance*
Joyce Carol Oates, *We Were the Mulvaneys*
Gwyn Hyman Rubio, *Icy Sparks*
Lalita Tademy, *Cane River*

2000 Isabelle Allende, *Daughter of Fortune*
Elizabeth Berg, *Open House*
Andre Dubus III, *House of Sand and Fog*
Barbara Kingsolver, *The Poisonwood Bible*
Sue Miller, *While I Was Gone*
Robert Morgan, *Gap Creek*
Toni Morrison, *The Bluest Eye*
Tawni O'Dell, *Back Roads*
Christina Schwarz, *Drowning Ruth*
1999 A. Manette Ansay, *Vinegar Hill*
Maeve Binchy, *Tara Road*
Breena Clarke, *River, Cross My Heart*
Janet Fitch, *White Oleander*
Melinda Haynes, *Mother of Pearl*
Jane Hamilton, *A Map of the World*
Bret Lott, *Jewel*
Bernhard Schlink, *The Reader*
Anita Shreve, *The Pilot's Wife*
1998 Chris Bohjalian, *Midwives*
Pearl Clage, *What Looks Like Crazy on an Ordinary Day*
Edwidge Danticat, *Breath, Eyes, Memory*
Alice Hoffman, *Here on Earth*
Wally Lamb, *I Know This Much Is True*
Billie Letts, *Where the Heart Is*
Toni Morrison, *Paradise*
Anna Quindlen, *Black and Blue*
1997 Ernest Gaines, *A Lesson Before Dying*
Kaye Gibbons, *Ellen Foster* and *A Virtuous Woman*
Ursula Hegi, *Stones from the River*
Wally Lamb, *She's Come Undone*
Mary McGarry Morris, *Songs in Ordinary Time*
Sheri Reynolds, *The Rapture of Canaan*
1996 Jane Hamilton, *The Book of Ruth*
Jacquelyn Mitchard, *The Deep End of the Ocean*
Toni Morrison, *The Song of Solomon*

☐ SOME ORIGINAL VOICES: FICTION

Since 1998 Borders has selected the "Best of the Original Voices Award" from books that are innovative and ambitious from new and emerging writers. Twenty-first-century fiction winners are:

2005 *The Shadow of the World* by Carlos Ruíz Zafón
2004 *The Kite Runner* by Khaled Hosseini
2003 *Book of Illusions* by Paul Auster
2002 *Ella Minnow Pea* by Mark Dunn
2001 *Bee Season* by Myla Goldberg
2000 *Close Range* by E. Annie Proulx

☐ CRITICS CHOICE – TWENTY-FIRST CENTURY

The National Book Critics Circle (comprised of more than seven hundred reviewers) annually selects books in five categories as the year's best. Here are the best since 2000 in fiction and general nonfiction:

Fiction	General Nonfiction
2004	
Marilynne Robinson *Gilead*	Diarmid MacCulloch, *The Reformation: A History*
2003	
Edward B. Jones, *The Known World*	Paul Hendrickson, *Sons of Mississippi: A Story of Race and Its Legacy*
2002	
Ian McEwan, *Atonement*	Samantha Power, *A Problem from Hell: America and the Age of Genocide*
2001	
W. G. Sebald, *Austerlitz*	Nicholson Baker, *Double Fold: Libraries and the Assault on Paper*
2000	
Jim Crace, *Being Dead*	Ted Conover, *Newjack: Guarding Sing Sing*

◻ SOME WRITERS WHO WENT TO NEW ENGLAND COLLEGES

Amherst

Henry Ward Beecher · Chris Bohjalian · Gerald Warner Brace · Dan Brown · Robert Brustein · Harlen Coben · Ted Conover · Melvil Dewey · Aaron Latham · William F. McFeely · James Merrill · Richard Poirier · William R. Pritchard · William G. Tapply · Scott Turow · David Foster Wallace · Richard Wilbur

Bates

John Ciardi · Owen Dodson · Elizabeth Strout

Bennington

Barbara Deming · Andrea Dworkin · Gretel Ehrlich · Jill Eisenstadt · Brett Easton Ellis · Laura Furman · Penelope Gilliatt · Jonathan Lethem · Cynthia MacDonald · Kathleen Norris · Roxanne Robinson · Liz Rosenberg · Donna Tartt · Anne Waldman · Alec Wilkinson

Boston University

Linda Barnes · Paul Beatty · Louise Bogan · Philip R. Craig · Peter Ho Davies · Allan Folsom · Nicholas Gage · Peter Guralnick · Ha Jin · Harry Kemelman · Jhumpa Lahiri · Mark Leyner · John L'Heureux · Craig Lucas · Elizabeth McCracken · Julia Marcus · Robert P. Parker · Kim Stanley Robinson · April Smith · Neal Stephenson

Bowdoin

Vance Bourjaily · Anthony Doerr · Nathaniel Hawthorne · Henry Wadsworth Longfellow · Lawrence Spingarn

Brandeis

Kathy Acker · Mitch Albom · Rosellen Brown · Richard Burgin · Anthony P. Dunbar · Thomas Friedman · Shirley Geok-Lin · Noah Gordon · Jeremy Larner · Alicia Ostriker · Linda Pastan · Letty Cottin Pogrebin · Alan Shapiro · Ronald Sukenick · Judith Thurman

Colby

Gerry Boyle · Doris Kearns Goodwin · Robert B. Parker · Frederick Pottle · Elizabeth Savage · Thomas Savage

Goddard

Piers Anthony · Roo Borson · Adam Braver · Mark Doty · Norman Dubie · Amy Hempel · David Mamet · Walter Mosley

Holy Cross

Billy Collins · Edward P. Jones · Joe McGinniss

Middlebury

Julia Alvarez · Mel Gussow · W. C. Heinz

Trinity

Edward Albee · Charles L. Grant · Ward Just · Naomi Shihab Nye · Hyam Plutzik

Tufts

Cid Corman · Barbara Delinsky · Christopher Golden · Jill Johnston · Bette Bao Lord · Mary Morris · Anita Shreve

University of Connecticut

Ann Beattie · David Gates · Wally Lamb · Bobbi Ann Mason · Ann Petry · Lewis Turco

University of Maine

Carolyn Chute · Bernd Heinrich · Stephen King · Tabitha King

University of Massachusetts

Andrea Barrett · Jack Canfield · Marilyn Chin · Suzanne Gardinier · Brett Lott · William Manchester · Valerie Martin · Susan Straight · Paul Theroux · Laura Zigman

University of New Hampshire

Shirley Frances Barker · Ursula Hegi · John Irving · Alice McDermott · Thomas Williams

University of Vermont

Burt Blechman · John Dewey · Lyn Lifshin · Mary McGarry Morris · E. Annie Proulx · Gail Sheehey

Wesleyan

Steve Almond · Amy Bloom · Rebecca Caudill · Robin Cook · Amanda Davis · Daniel Handler (AKA Lemony Snicket) · Kaylie Jones · Sebastian Junger · Pagan Kennedy · Alex Kotlowitz · Robert Ludlum · Charles Olson · Carolyn Parkhurst · Stephen Schiff · John Seelye · Ayelet Waldman · Simone Zelitch

Williams

Peter Abrahams · Bernard Bailyn · Michael Beschloss · Stephen Birmingham · Sterling Brown · David MacGregor Burns · Dominic Dunne · A. B. Gurney, Jr. · Walter Kauffman · Elia Kazan · Joseph McElroy · Jay McInerney · I. E. Modesitt, Jr. · Noel Perrin · John Sayles · Stephen Sondheim · John Toland

---

☐ OLDEST PROFESSIONAL SOCIETY OF AUTHORS

Founded in 1919, the Authors Guild is America's oldest and largest professional society of published authors. It lobbies for free speech, copyrights, and other issues of concern to authors.

☐ SOME UNIVERSITY OF CHICAGO GRADUATES

Allan Bloom · Ana Castillo · Henry Steele Commager · Will Cuppy · Vardis Fisher · Martin Gardner · Jean Garrigue · Andrew M. Greeley · John Gunther · Seymour M. Hersh · Bette Howland · Janet Kaufmann · Stephen Leacock · Fritz Leiber · Janet Lewis · Norman Maclean · Sara Paretsky · Robert Pirsig · Elizabeth Madox Roberts · M. L. Rosenthal · Leo Rosten · Philip Roth · Susan Sontag · George Steiner · Studs Terkel · Douglas Unger · Carl Van Vechten · Kurt Vonnegut, Jr.

□ POETS LAUREATE OF THE UNITED STATES

Ted Kooser	2004
Louise Glück	2003–04
Billy Collins	2001–03
Stanley Kunitz	2000–01
Robert Pinsky	1997–2000
Robert Hass	1995–97
Rita Dove	1993–95
Mona Van Duyn	1992–93
Joseph Brodsky	1991–92
Mark Strand	1990–91
Howard Nemerov	1988–90
Richard Wilbur	1987–88
Robert Penn Warren	1966–87

□ BOLLINGEN PRIZE IN POETRY

Among the most prestigious prizes available to American poets, the Bollingen Prize has, for more than a half century, been a force in shaping contemporary American letters.

Léonie Adams · Conrad Aiken · A. A. Ammons · John Ashbery · W. H. Auden · John Berryman · Louise Bogan · Edgar Bowers · Fred Chappell · Robert Creeley · E. E. Cummings · Richard Eberhardt · Robert Frost · Louise Glück · Horace Gregory · Anthony Hecht · John Hollander · David Ignatow · Laura Riding Jackson · Donald Justice · Kenneth Koch · Stanley Kunitz · Archibald MacLeish · James Merrill · W. S. Merwin · Marianne Moore · Howard Nemerov · Ezra Pound · John Crowe Ransom · Adrienne Rich · Theodore Roethke · Delmore Schwartz · Karl Shapiro · Gary Snyder · Wallace Stevens · Mark Strand · May Swenson · Allen Tate · Mona Van Duyn · Robert Penn Warren · John Hall Wheelock · Richard Wilbur · William Carlos Williams · Yvor Winters · Jay Wright

☐ MULTIPLE WINNERS OF THE PULITZER PRIZE (POETRY)

Stephen Vincent Benét (2) · Robert Frost (4) · Robert Lowell (2) · Archibald MacLeish (2) · Edward Arlington Robinson (3) · Robert Penn Warren (2) · Richard Wilbur (2)

☐ SOME KNOPF WRITERS

Alfred A. Knopf (1892–1984) started his eponymous publishing firm in 1915. Over the years he published some of the premier writers of his time, including:

Elizabeth Bowen · Albert Camus · T. S. Eliot · Sigmund Freud · Langston Hughes · Franz Kafka · D. H. Lawrence · Thomas Mann · H. L. Mencken · John Updike

---

☐ SOME NOTRE DAME ALUMNI

Robert Sam Anson · Michael Collins · Dan Coyle · Joe Gores · Barry Lopez · John Frederick Nims · Nicholas Sparks · James Ellis Thomas

---

☐ SOME H. L. MENCKEN QUOTATIONS

I never lecture, not because I am shy or a bad speaker, but simply because I detest the kind of people who go to lectures and don't want to meet them.

It is the dull man who is always sure, and the sure man who is always dull.

Nobody ever went broke underestimating the taste of the American public.

Love is the triumph of imagination over intelligence,

Conscience is the inner voice that warns us somebody may be looking.

We are here and it is now. Further than that all human knowledge is moonshine.

H. L. MENCKEN

An idealist is one who, on noticing that a rose smells better than a cabbage, concludes that it will also make better soup.

A cynic is a man who, when he smells flowers, looks around for a coffin.

A celebrity is one who is known to many persons he is glad he doesn't know.

It is inaccurate to say that I hate everything. I am strongly in favor of common sense, common honesty, and common decency. This makes me forever ineligible for public office.

Criticism is prejudice made plausible.

Puritanism: The haunting fear that someone, somewhere, may be happy.

The chief value of money lies in the fact that one lives in a world in which it is overestimated.

The older I grow the more I distrust the familiar doctrine that age brings wisdom.

The difference between a moral man and a man of honor is that the latter regrets a discreditable act, even when it has worked, and he has not been caught.

The whole aim of practical politics is to keep the populace alarmed (and hence clamorous to be led to safety) by menacing it with an endless series of hobgoblins, all of them imaginary.

□ NATIONAL HISTORIC LANDMARKS ASSOCIATED WITH LITERARY FIGURES

National Historic Landmarks are nationally significant historic places designated by the secretary of the interior because they possess exceptional value in illustrating the heritage of the United States.

Jack London Ranch, *Sonoma County, California*
Joaquin Miller House, *Oakland, California*
John Muir House, *Martinez, California*

Frank Norris Cabin, *Santa Clara County, California*
Upton Sinclair House, *Monrovia, California*
Mark Twain Home, *Hartford, Connecticut*
Noah Webster Birthplace, *Hartford, Connecticut*
Ernest Hemingway House, *Key West, Florida*
Zora Neale Hurston House, *Fort Pierce, Florida*
Stephen Vincent Benét House, *Augusta, Georgia*
Joel Chandler Harris House, *Atlanta, Georgia*
Vachel Lindsay House, *Springfield, Illinois*
James Whitcomb Riley House, *Indianapolis, Indiana*
George Washington Cable House, *New Orleans, Louisiana*
Kate Chopin House, *Cloutierville, Louisiana*
Sarah Orne Jewett House, *South Berwick, Maine*
Edwin Arlington Robinson House, *Gardiner, Maine*
Harriet Beecher Stowe House, *Brunswick, Maine*
Wadsworth-Longfellow House, *Portland, Maine*
Rachel Carson House, *Silver Springs, Maryland*
H. L. Mencken House, *Baltimore, Maryland*
Edgar Allan Poe House, *Baltimore, Maryland*
Edward Bellamy House, *Chicopee Falls, Massachusetts*
Brook Farm, *West Roxbury, Massachusetts*
William Cullen Bryant Homestead, *Cummington, Massachusetts*
Emily Dickinson Home, *Amherst, Massachusetts*
W. E. B. Du Bois Boyhood Homesite, *Great Barrington, Massachusetts*
Ralph Waldo Emerson Home, *Concord, Massachusetts*
Margaret Fuller House, *Cambridge, Massachusetts*
Oliver Wendell Holmes House, *Beverly, Massachusetts*
Longfellow House, *Cambridge, Massachusetts*
Francis Parkman House, *Boston, Massachusetts*
William H. Prescott House, *Boston, Massachusetts*
Walden Pond, *Middlesex County, Massachusetts*
The Wayside "Home of Authors," *Concord, Massachusetts*
John Greenleaf Whittier Home, *Amesbury, Massachusetts*
Ernest Hemingway Cottage, *Emmet County, Michigan*
F. Scott Fitzgerald House, *St. Paul, Minnesota*
Sinclair Lewis Boyhood Home, *Sauk Centre, Minnesota*

William Faulkner House, *Oxford, Mississippi*
Mark Twain Boyhood Home, *Hannibal, Missouri*
Laura Ingalls Wilder House, *Mansfield, Missouri*
Willa Cather House, *Red Cloud, Nebraska*
e. e. cummings House, *Silver Lake, New Hampshire*
Robert Frost Homestead, *Rockingham, New Hampshire*
Walt Whitman House, *Camden, New Jersey*
James Weldon Johnson Residence, *New York, New York*
Claude McKay Residence, *New York, New York*
Thomas Wolfe House, *Asheville, North Carolina*
Paul Laurence Dunbar House, *Dayton, Ohio*
Pearl S. Buck House, *Bucks County, Pennsylvania*
Edgar Allan Poe House, *Philadelphia, Pennsylvania*
Dubose Heyward House, *Charleston, South Carolina*
Robert Frost Farm, *Addison County, Vermont*
Ellen Glasgow House, *Richmond, Virginia*
Hamlin Garland House, *West Salem, Wisconsin*

☐ RANDOM HOUSE

Started by Bennett Cerf in 1927, two years after he and Donald Klopfer acquired the Modern Library imprint. Published *Ulysses* in the U.S. in 1934. Among its authors have been Truman Capote, John O'Hara, Irwin Shaw, Eugene O'Neill, and James A. Michener.

☐ SOME NORTHEASTERN COLLEGE STUDENTS

American University

Ann Beattie · Joanne Greenberg · Barry Levinson · Carolyn Parkhurst

Bard

Olga Carlisle · Phyllis Chesler · Laurie Colwin · Rikki Ducornet · David Gates · Anthony Hecht · John Katzenbach

Bucknell

Peter Balakian · Susan Dunlap · David Nasaw · Philip Roth

Fordham

Tom Cahill · Mary Higgins Clark · Robert Daley · Ed Dee · Don DeLillo · Thomas Fleming · Lev Raphael · Robert V. Remini · Valerie Sayers

Georgetown

William Peter Blatty · Douglas Brinkley · Margaret Edson · John Guare · Mark Jude Poirier · David Schickler

Hamilton

Peter Cameron · Terry Brooks · Thomas Meehan · John Nichols · Ezra Pound · Kamila Shamsie · B. F. Skinner · Alexander Woollcott

Haverford

Nicholson Baker · Dave Barry · John Dickson Carr · Frank Conroy · Colin Harrison · Christopher Morley

Hofstra

Nelson DeMille · Stephen Dunn · Marilyn French · Dennis Lynds

Howard

Amiri Baraka · Ossie Davis · John Oliver Killens · Omar Tyree

Johns Hopkins

Russell Baker · John Barth · Frederick Barthelme · Lucie Brock Broido · Rachel Carson · Richard Ben Cramer · Benjamin DeMott · Cristina García · Philip Hamburger · Murray Kempton · Wayne Koestenbaum · Earl Lovelace · James McPherson · P. J. O'Rourke · Mary Robison · Gil Scott-Heron

New York University

Warren Adler · Courtney Angela Brkic · Rita Mae Brown · Countee Cullen · Laura Shaine Cunningham · Thomas Disch · Stephen Dixon · Leslie Fiedler · Arthur Golden · Vivian Gornick · Jorie Graham · Jean Harfenist · Stefan Kanfer · Stanley Kauffmann · Ira Levin · James McCourt · Leonard Michaels · Albert Murray · John Ridley · Kerri Sakamoto · Laurence

Shames · John Patrick Shanley · Robert Sheckley · Charles Simic · Danielle Steel · Robert Stone · Darrin Strauss · Jerome Weidman · Howard Zinn

RUTGERS

Jonathan Carroll · Alan Cheuse · Fred S. Cook · Digby Diehl · Henry Dumas · Janice Evanovich · Jeremiah Healy · Joyce Kilmer · Peter Najarian · Alan E. Nourse · Robert Pinsky · Michael Shaara · Judith Viorst

SARAH LAWRENCE

Patricia Bosworth · Melvyn Jules Bukiet · Carolyn Ferrell · Leslie Glass · Allan Gurganus · Lauren Hillenbrand · Ken Kalfus · Carolyn Kizer · Heather Lewis · Myra Cohn Livingston · Brian Morton · Ann Packer · Ann Patchett · Anne Roiphe · Joan Silber · Dorothea Straus · Alice Walker · Elizabeth Winthrop

SWARTHMORE

T. Alan Broughton · Jonathan Franzen · Adam Haslett · James Michener · Joyce Milton · Hugh Nissenson · Rudy Rucker · Norman Rush · Roger Sale

SYRACUSE

Julia Alvarez · Ken Auletta · George C. Chesbro · Stephen Crane · Adam Desnoyers · Guy Davenport · William DeAndrea · Stephen Dunn · Richard Elman · Mary Gordon · Clement Greenberg · Stanley Edgar Hyman · Shirley Jackson · Hilton Kramer · Greg Kuzma · Janice Law · Larry Levis · Lyn Lifshin · David Liss · John D. MacDonald · Michael Malone · Barry Malzberg · Norma Fox Mazer · Drew Middleton · Howard Frank Mosher · Joyce Carol Oates · Tom Perotta · William Safire · Alice Sebold · Laura Van Wormer · Paul Watkins · John A. Williams

UNIVERSITY OF MARYLAND

Joan Chase · Rosario Ferre · Martha Grimes · Joe Haldeman · Karen Hesse · Munro Leaf · Michael Mewshaw · George Pelecanos

□ NEW YORK STATE AUTHOR AND STATE POET

The New York State Writers Institute of the State University of New York awards both the Edith Wharton Citation of Merit for fiction writers (State Author) and the Walt Whitman Citation of Merit for poets (State Poet) every two years. Each citation carries an honorarium of $10,000 and requires that the recipients "shall promote and encourage fiction and poetry within the State and shall give two public readings within the State each year."

Year	State Author	State Poet
2004–06	Russell Banks	Billy Collins
2001–03	Kurt Vonnegut	John Ashbery
1998–2000	James Salter	Sharon Olds
1995–97	Peter Matthiessen	Jane Cooper
1993–95	William Gaddis	Richard Howard
1991–93	Norman Mailer	Audre Lorde
1989–91	E. L. Doctorow	Robert Creeley
1986–88	Grace Paley	Stanley Kunitz

□ HARCOURT BRACE & COMPANY

In 1919 two former Henry Holt & Co. employees, Alfred Harcourt and Donald Brace, founded their new company, bringing with them from Holt authors Sinclair Lewis and Carl Sandburg.

Over the years, Harcourt expanded to include many notable authors, such as Lytton Strachey, Virginia Woolf, George Orwell, C. S. Lewis, William Golding, Stephen Spender, Dorothy Sayers, Kingsley Amis, Arthur C. Clarke, Cyril Connolly, Thomas Merton, Robert Lowell, and Eudora Welty. Copublishers Helen and Kurt Wolff, cofounders of Pantheon, joined the company, and brought with them such international authors as Günter Grass, Hannah Arendt, and Konrad Lorenz. Hiram Hadyn, a cofounder of the former Atheneum, also brought along new authors such as Anaïs Nin and Alice Walker.

☐ SOME WHITING WRITERS

Sponsored by the Mrs. Giles Whiting Foundation, the Whiting Writers Award ($35,000) has been given annually since 1985 to ten emerging writers of "exceptional talent and promise" in fiction, nonfiction, poetry, and drama.

Kirsten Bakis · Michael Cunningham · Mark Doty · Deborah Eisenberg · Jeffrey Eugenides · Jonathan Franzen · Dagoberto Gilb · Allegra Goodman · Richard Hugo · Michelle Huneven · Mary Karr · Tony Kushner · Victor LaValle · Alice McDermott · Z. Z. Packer · Katha Pollitt · Mona Simpson · William T. Vollmann · David Foster Wallace · Colson Whitehead

---

☐ BEST SHORT STORY WRITERS

The PEN/Malamud Award has been given since 1988 in recognition of a body of work that demonstrates excellence in the art of short fiction. In recent years it has been awarded jointly to one established writer and one at the beginning of a literary career:

2005 Lorrie Moore
2004 Richard Bausch & Nell Freudenberger
2003 Barry Hannah & Maile Meloy
2002 Ursula K. Le Guin & Junot Díaz
2001 Richard Ford & Sherman Alexie
2000 Ann Beattie & Nathan Englander
1999 T. Coraghessan Boyle
1998 John Barth
1997 Alice Munro
1996 Joyce Carol Oates
1995 William Maxwell & Stuart Dybek
1994 Grace Paley
1993 Peter Taylor
1992 Eudora Welty
1991 Frederick Busch & Andre Dubus
1990 George Garrett
1989 Saul Bellow
1988 John Updike

☐ TOP WORKS OF JOURNALISM IN THE UNITED STATES

The New York University journalism faculty and a special panel of distinguished journalists selected the top one hundred works of journalism in the United States in the twentieth century. The list included magazine articles, radio, and television dispatches, as well as books. The top ten books were:

1. *Hiroshima* by John Hersey (1946)
2. *Silent Spring* by Rachel Carson (1962)
3. *Ten Days That Shook the World* by John Reed (1919)
4. *Let Us Now Praise Famous Men* by James Agee and Walker Evans (1941)
5. *The Souls of Black Folk* by W. E. B. Du Bois (1903)
6. *Eyes on the Prize* by Henry Hampton (1987)
7. *Electric Kool-Aid Acid Test* by Tom Wolfe (1968)
8. *The Armies of the Night* by Norman Mailer (1968)
9. *Eichmann in Jerusalem* by Hannah Arendt (1963)
10. *Berlin Diary* by William Shirer (1941)

☐ NBCC AWARD: BIOGRAPHY/AUTOBIOGRAPHY

Since 1983, the National Book Critics Circle has selected the best biography or autobiography of the year:

2004 *De Kooning: An American Master* by Mark Stevens & Annalyn Swan
2003 *Khruschev* by William Taubman
2002 *Charles Darwin: The Power of Place*, Vol. II by Janet Browne
2001 *Boswell's Presumptuous Task: The Making of the Life of Dr. Johnson* by Adam Sisman
2000 *Hirohito and the Making of Modern Japan* by Herbert P. Bix
1999 *The Hairstons: An American Family in Black and White* by Henry Wiencek
1998 *A Beautiful Mind* by Sylvia Nasar
1997 *Ernie Pyle's War: America's Eyewitness to World War II* by James Tobin

1996 *Angela's Ashes* by Frank McCourt
1995 *Savage Art: A Biography of Jim Thompson* by Robert Polito
1994 *Shot in the Heart* by Mikal Gilmore
1993 *Genet* by Edmund White
1992 *Writing Dangerously: Mary McCarthy and Her World* by Carol Brightman
1991 *Patrimony: A True Story* by Philip Roth
1990 *Means of Ascent: The Years of Lyndon Johnson*, Vol. 2 by Robert A. Caro
1989 *A First Class Temperament: The Emergence of Franklin Roosevelt* by Geoffrey C. Ward
1988 *Oscar Wilde* by Richard Ellmann
1987 *Chaucer: His Life, His Works, His World* by Donald R. Howard
1986 *Tombee: Portrait of a Cotton Planter* by Theodore Rosengarten
1985 *Henry James: A Life* by Leon Edel
1984 *Dostoevsky: The Years of Ordeal, 1850–1859* by Joseph Frank
1983 *Minor Characters* by Joyce Johnson

□ WRITERS IN THE LIBRARY OF AMERICA

The Library of America was founded in 1979 to help preserve the nation's cultural heritage by publishing America's most significant writing in authoritative editions. To date, the following authors have had a volume or volumes of their own:

Henry Adams · John James Audubon · James Baldwin · William Bartram · Saul Bellow · Paul Bowles · Charles Brockden Brown · Raymond Chandler · Charles W. Chesnutt · Kate Chopin · James Fenimore Cooper · Stephen Crane · John Dos Passos · Frederick Douglass · Theodore Dreiser · W. E. B. Du Bois · Ralph Waldo Emerson · James T. Farrell · William Faulkner · F. Scott Fitzgerald · Benjamin Franklin · Robert Frost · Ulysses S. Grant · Alexander Hamilton · Dashiell Hammett · Nathaniel Hawthorne · William Dean Howells · Zora Neale Hurston · Washington Irving · Henry James · William James · Thomas Jefferson · Sarah Orne

Jewett · James Weldon Johnson · George S. Kaufman & Co. · Sinclair Lewis · Abraham Lincoln · Jack London · H. P. Lovecraft · Henry Wadsworth Longfellow · James Madison · Carson McCullers · Herman Melville · John Muir · Vladimir Nabokov · Flannery O'Connor · Eugene O'Neill · Thomas Paine · Edgar Allan Poe · Ezra Pound · Dawn Powell · Theodore Roosevelt · Philip Roth · William T. Sherman · Isaac Bashevis Singer · Gertrude Stein · John Steinbeck · Wallace Stevens · Harriet Beecher Stowe · Henry David Thoreau · James Thurber · Alexis de Tocqueville · Mark Twain · George Washington · Eudora Welty · Nathanael West · Edith Wharton · Walt Whitman · Tennessee Williams · Richard Wright

---

□ THE BULWER-LYTTON CONTEST

A literary parody contest, the competition honors the memory, if not the reputation, of Victorian novelist Edward George Earl Bulwer-Lytton (1803-1873). Entrants are challenged to submit a bad opening sentences to imaginary novels." (www.bulwer-lytton.com) Some of the past winners:

2003: They had but one last remaining night together, so they embraced each other as tightly as that two-flavor entwined string cheese that is orange and yellowish-white, the orange probably being a bland Cheddar and the white . . . Mozzarella, although it could possibly be a Provolone or just plain American, as it really doesn't taste distinctly dissimilar from the orange, yet they would have you believe it does by coloring it differently.

– Marianne Simms

2001: A small assortment of astonishingly loud brass instruments raced each other lustily to the respective ends of their distinct musical choices as the gates flew open to release a torrent of tawny fur comprised of angry yapping bullets that nipped at Desdemona's ankles, causing her to reflect once again (as blood filled her sneakers and she fought her way through the panicking crowd) that the annual Running of The Pomeranians in Liechtenstein was a stupid idea. – Sera Kirk

1999: Through the gathering gloom of a late-October afternoon, along the greasy, cracked paving-stones slick from the sputum of the sky, Stanley Ruddlethorp wearily trudged up the hill from the cemetery where his wife, sister, brother, and three children were all buried, and forced open the door of his decaying house, blissfully unaware of the catastrophe that was soon to devastate his life. – Dr. David Chuter

1991: Sultry it was and humid, but no whisper of air caused the plump, laden spears of golden grain to nod their burdened heads as they unheedingly awaited the cyclic rape of their gleaming treasure, while overhead the burning orb of luminescence ascended its ever-upward path toward a sweltering celestial apex, for although it is not in Kansas that our story takes place, it looks godawful like it. – Judy Frazier

---

☐ BEST IN AMERICAN NONFICTION

The J. Anthony Lukas Book Prize, administered by the Columbia University Graduate School of Journalism and the Nieman Foundation for Journalism at Harvard University, honors the best in American socially concerned nonfiction writing.

2005 *Generation Kill: Devil Dogs, Iceman, Captain America, and the New Face of American War* by Evan Wright
2004 *They Marched into Sunlight: War and Peace, Vietnam and America* by David Maraniss
2003 *A Problem from Hell: America and the Age of Genocide* by Samantha Power
2002 *Carry Me Home: Birmingham, Alabama, The Climactic Battle of the Civil Rights Revolution* by Diane McWhorter
2001 *The Chief: The Life of William Randolph Hearst* by David Nasaw
2000 *A Clearing in the Distance: Frederick Law Olmstead and America in the Nineteenth Century* by Witold Rybczynski
1999 *All on Fire: William Lloyd Garrison and the Abolition of Slavery* by Henry Mayer

◻ SOME FORMER STUDENTS OF SOUTHERN UNIVERSITIES

AUBURN

Ace Atkins · Paul Hemphill · Lewis Nordan · Anne River Siddons

DUKE

Fred Chappell · Guy Davenport · John Feinstein · Josephine Humphreys · Charlie Smith · William Styron · Anne Tyler

EMORY

Alfred Corn · Carl Hiaasen · Dumas Malone · Ferrol Sams · C. Vann Woodward

FISK

William Demby · W. E. B. Du Bois · John Hope Franklin · Nikki Giovanni · Nella Larsen · Melvin B. Tolson · Frank Yerby

HOLLINS

Madison Smart Bell · Margaret Wise Brown · Annie Dillard · Elizabeth Forsythe · Hailey David Huddle · Tama Janowitz · Jill McCorkle · Shannon Ravenel · Lee Smith

LOUISIANA STATE

Stephen E. Ambrose · John Ed Bradley · Robb Dew · Thomas McGrath · Rex Reed · Olympia Vernon · Allen Wier

TULANE

Hamilton Basso · Richard Bradford · Cleanth Brooks · Shirley Ann Grau · Isabelle Holland · Evelyn Scott · John Kennedy Toole · Steven Womack

UNIVERSITY OF ALABAMA

Mark Childress · Tony Earley · Fannie Flagg · Winston Groom · Andrew Hudgins · Rodney Jones · Harper Lee · Robert R. McCammon · Barbara Park · Edward O. Wilson

UNIVERSITY OF ARKANSAS

Lee K. Abbott · John Dufresne · Barry Hannah · Joan Hess · Ellen Gilchrist · Donald Harington · E. Lynn Harris · Douglas Jones · Charles Portis · Steven Stern · Gay Talese · C. D. Wright

University of Florida

Wendy Brenner · Rita Mae Brown · Kevin Canty · Archie Carr · Michael Connelly · Harry Crews · Lolita Files · Joan Gerber · Carl Hiaasen · Jesse Hill · Frances Mayes · Ford Merrill · Meredith Ann Pierce · Celestine Sibley

University of Georgia

Michael Bishop · Tom Deitz · Lewis Grizzard · Stuart Woods

University of Kentucky

Wendell Berry · Harry Caudill · Elizabeth Hardwick · Bobbie Ann Mason · Karen Robards · Walter Tevis

University of Mississippi

Larry Brown · Ellen Douglas · William Faulkner · John Grisham · Greg Iles · Julie Smith · Donna Tartt · Steve Yarbrough

University of North Carolina

Russell Banks · Doris Betts · Edgar Bowers · Taylor Branch · Poppy Z. Brite · Davis Burke · Olive Ann Burns · Hayden Carruth · Pam Durban · Clyde Edgerton · John Ehle · Lawrence Ferlinghetti · Shelby Foote · Charles Frazier · Kaye Gibbons · Gail Godwin · Jim Grimsley · Mary Hood · Donald Justice · Lily King · Brad Land · Jill McCorkle · Sharyn McCrumb · Armistead Maupin · Joseph Mitchell · Robert Morgan · Walker Percy · Leon Rooke · Robert Ruark · Max Steele · Richard G. Stern · Tom Wicker · Thomas Wolfe

University of South Carolina

Charles Frazier · Tim Gautreaux · Sarah Gilbert

University of Tennessee

Joseph Wood Krutch · David Madden · Cormac McCarthy · Walter M. Miller

University of Virginia

Louis Auchincloss · David Baldacci · Stringfellow Barr · Paul Bowles · Rebecca Brown · Matthew Bruccoli · Erskine Caldwell ·

Martin Clark · Linda Fairstein · Stephen W. Frey · Julien Green · David Huddle · Edward P. Jones · Breece D'J Pancake · Edgar Allan Poe · Karl Shapiro · Alexander Theroux

VANDERBILT UNIVERSITY

Roy Blount, Jr. · Cleanth Brooks · Rebecca Caudill · Brainard Cheney · Walter Van Tilburg Clark · James Dickey · Ellen Gilchrist · Caroline Gordon · Randall Jarrell · Madison Jones · Andrew Lytle · Merrill Moore · James Patterson · Susan Richards Shreve · Elizabeth Spencer · James Still · Jesse Stuart · Allen Tate · Robert Penn Warren

WAKE FOREST

Stephen Amidon · A. R. Ammons · W. J. Cash

WEST VIRGINIA UNIVERSITY

Ann Pancake · Stephen Coonts · Keith Maillard · Jayne Anne Phillips · Melville Davison Post · Sara Vogan

---

□ SOME SOUTHERN NOVELS

The Southern Book Awards have been presented annually since 1991 by the Southern Book Critics Circle. Some of the past fiction award winners are:

Doris Betts, *Souls Raised from the Dead*
Larry Brown, *Joe and Father and Son*
Connie May Fowler, *Before Women Had Wings*
Charles Frazier, *Cold Mountain*
Alan Gurganus, *The Oldest Living Confederate Widow Tells All*
Josephine Humphreys, *Nowhere Else on Earth*
Edward P. Jones, *The Known World*
Bobbie Ann Mason, *Feather Crowns* and *Zigzagging Down a Wild Trail*
Robert Morgan, *Gap Creek*
Lee Smith, *The Last Girls*
Brad Watson, *The Heaven of Mercury*

☐ THE GEORGIA WRITERS HALL OF FAME

Established by the University of Georgia Libraries in 2000, it singles out writers associated with Georgia for inclusion in its literary hall of fame:

Conrad Aiken · Elias Boudinot · Erskine Caldwell · Harry Crews · James Dickey · W. E. B. Du Bois · Joel Chandler Harris · John Oliver Killens · Martin Luther King, Jr. · Sidney Lanier · Augustus B. Longstreet · Carson McCullers · Margaret Mitchell · Flannery O'Connor · Byron Herbert Reece · Lillian Smith · Jean Toomer · Alice Walker

---

☐ SOME CONTEMPORARY AUTHORS FROM NORTH CAROLINA

Doris Betts · Betsy Byars · Fred Chappell · Tony Earley · Clyde Edgerton · Charles Frazier · Kaye Gibbons · Gail Godwin · Alan Gurganus · Jan Karon · Jill McCorkle · Sharyn McCrumb · Michael Malone · Margaret Maron · Robert Morgan · T. R. Pearson · Reynolds Price · Tom Robbins · David Sedaris · Lionel Shriver · Lee Smith · June Spence · Anne Tyler

---

☐ BEST GOLF NOVELS

According to the resident golf maven at www.about.com, these are the ten best:

1. *The Greatest Player Who Never Played* by J. Michael Veron
2. *Dead Solid Perfect* by Dan Jenkins
3. *Missing Links* by Rick Reilly
4. *On a Par with Murder* by John Logue
5. *The Green* by Troon McAllister
6. *Fast Greens* by Turk Pipkin
7. *A Mulligan for Bobby Jobe* by Robert Cullen
8. *Mr. Ryder's Trophy* by Shirley Dusinberre Durham
9. *The Greatest Course That Never Was* by J. Michael Veron
10. *The Foursome* by Troon McAllister

ALICE WALKER

☐ BEST SPORTS BOOKS OF ALL TIME

The first ten from the Sports Illustrated *2002 list of the Top 100 Sports Books of All Time*

1. A. J. Liebling, *The Sweet Science* (1956)
2. Roger Kahn, *The Boys of Summer* (1971)
3. Jim Bouton, *Ball Four* (1970)
4. H. G. Bissinger, *Friday Night Lights* (1990)
5. Ring Lardner, *You Know Me Al* (1914)
6. John Feinstein, *A Season on the Brink* (1986)
7. Dan Jenkins, *Semi-Tough* (1972)
8. George Plimpton, *Paper Lion* (1965)
9. Ken Dryden, *The Game* (1983)
10. Nick Hornby, *Fever Pitch* (1991)

☐ BEST BASEBALL NOVELS

These were the only baseball novels to appear among the Sports Illustrated Top 100 Sports Books.

Ring Lardner, *You Know Me Al* (1914)
Mark Harris, *Bang the Drum Slowly* (1956)
Bernard Malamud, *The Natural* (1952)
Eric Rolfe Greenberg, *The Celebrant* (1983)
W. P. Kinsella, *Shoeless Joe* (1982)
Robert Coover, *The Universal Baseball Association, Inc.* (1968)
Philip Roth, *The Great American Novel* (1973)
William Brashler, *The Bingo Long Traveling All-Stars and Motor Kings* (1973)

☐ BEST BOOKS ABOUT BASKETBALL

Hoops books selected by Sports Illustrated *editors for their Top 100 Sports Books list.*

Terry Pluto, *Loose Balls* (1990)
Pete Axthelm, *The City Game* (1970)
Stanley Cohen, *The Game They Played* (1977)

Bill Bradley, *Life on the Run* (1976)
David Wolf, *Foul! The Connie Hawkins Story* (1972)
John Wooden with Jack Tobin, *They Call Me Coach* (1972)
Alexander Wolff, *Big Game, Small World* (2002)
Darcy Frey, *The Last Shot* (1994)

☐ DOUBLEDAY

In 1880, eighteen-year-old Frank Nelson Doubleday went to work at Scribner's. Feuding with Scribner led Doubleday to quit and begin his own company. When news got around, publisher S. S. McClure offered him a partnership, to be called Doubleday, McClure & Co. Doubleday contacted his friend, Rudyard Kipling, who promised to let the new company publish his next books. In 1900 Doubleday ended the partnership with McClure to begin one with Walter Hines Page. Doubleday brought to this new partnership most of the titles and authors he had acquired at Doubleday, McClure & Co., including Mark Twain. In 1908, McClure decided to retire, so he offered his firm to Doubleday, who quickly agreed to purchase it. Authors who came from McClure include Joseph Conrad, Booth Tarkington, Arthur Conan Doyle, Stewart Edward White, and Kate Douglas Wiggins.

☐ SOME WRITERS EDITED BY MAXWELL PERKINS

Probably the most famous editor of the twentieth century, Perkins (1884–1947) spent thirty-seven years at Scribner's when it published some of the best American writers of the time.

Sherwood Anderson · Vance Bourjaily · Ernest Hemingway · F. Scott Fitzgerald · James Jones · Ring Lardner · Dawn Powell · Marjorie Kinnan Rawlings · Thomas Wolfe

---

☐ FIRST PUBLISHED NOVEL BY AN AFRICAN AMERICAN WRITER

Clotelle (1853) by William Wells Brown

☐ BEST AFRICAN AMERICAN NOVELS

The BCALA Literary Award is given annually by the Black Caucus of the American Library Association for outstanding works by African American authors.

2005 Diane McKinney-Whetstone, *Leaving Cecil Street*
2004 Barbara Chase-Riboud, *Hottentot Venus*
2003 Jewell Parker Rhodes, *Douglass' Women*
2002 Pearl Cleage, *I Wish I Had a Red Dress*
2001 Paule Marshall, *The Fisher King*
2000 Valerie Wilson Wesley, *Ain't Nobody's Business If I Do*
1999 Gayl Jones, *The Healing*
1998 Sandra Jackson-Opoku, *The River Where Blood Is Born*
1997 Florence Ladd, *Sarah's Psalm*
1996 Walter Mosley, *RL's Dream*
1995 Maxine Clair, *Rattlebone*
1994 Ernest J. Gaines, *A Lesson Before Dying*

☐ THE HOWELLS MEDAL

Conferred every five years by the American Academy and Institute of Arts and Letters in recognition of the most distinguished work of American fiction during that period (prior to 1955 it was made for the recipient's body of work).

2000 Don DeLillo, *Underworld*
1995 John Updike, *Rabbit at Rest*
1990 E. L. Doctorow, *Billy Bathgate*
1985 No award
1980 William Maxwell *So Long, See You Tomorrow*
1975 Thomas Pynchon, *Gravity's Rainbow*
1970 William Styron, *The Confessions of Nat Turner*
1965 John Cheever, *The Wapshot Chronicle*
1960 James Gould Cozzens, *By Love Possessed*
1955 Eudora Welty, *The Ponder Heart*
1950 William Faulkner
1945 Booth Tarkington
1940 Ellen Glasgow
1935 Pearl S. Buck

1930 Willa Cather
1925 Mary E. Wilkins Freeman

□ FAVORITE AFRICAN AMERICAN NOVELS OF THE TWENTIETH CENTURY

The African American Literary Book Club list of one hundred favorite African American novels of the twentieth century was made by visitors to its Web site, and does not reflect formal judging criteria.

1. Alice Walker, *The Color Purple*
2. Zora Neale Hurston, *Their Eyes Were Watching God*
3. Toni Morrison, *Beloved*
4. E. Lynn Harris, *And This Too Shall Pass*
5. Maya Angelou, *I Know Why the Caged Bird Sings*
6. J. California Cooper, *Some Love, Some Pain, Some Time: Stories*
7. Terry McMillan, *Disappearing Acts*
8. Ralph Ellison, *Invisible Man*
9. Toni Morrison, *Song of Solomon*
10. Richard Wright, *Native Son*

□ SOME FORMER "BIG TEN" STUDENTS

Indiana University

Elliot Baker · Robert Coover · John Crowley · Theodore Dreiser · Clayton Eshleman · William Ernie Pyle · Lucien Stryk · Judy Troy · David Wagoner · Dan Wakefield · Harvey Wheeler · Marguerite Young

Michigan State University

Thomas Adcock · Carolyn Forché · Richard Ford · Gary Gildner · Jim Harrison · Thomas McGuane · Alexei Panshin · Joe Poyer · Vernon Vinge · Theodore Weesner · Kate Wilhelm · Timothy Zahn

Northwestern University

Saul Bellow · Robert Olen Butler · Ivan Doig · Wilma Dykeman ·

Timothy Ferris · Bob Greene · Stephen Hunter · Walter Kerr · Laura Lippman · George R. R. Martin · James Mellow · Tawni O'Dell · Neal Pollack · J. F. Powers · Kathy Reichs · Sidney Sheldon · Terry Southern · Kate Walbert · Margaret Walker

Ohio State University

Lois McMaster Bujold · Kenneth Burke · W. S. Burnett · Jennifer Crusie · Harlan Ellison · Dorothy Canfield Fisher · Vicki Hendricks · Chester Himes · John Jakes · Jerome Lawrence · Lois Lenski · Cynthia Ozick · R. L. Stine · James Thurber · Thrity Umrigar · Stephanie Vaughan

Purdue University

George Ade · George Harmon Coxe · Mercedes R. Lackey · Booth Tarkington

University of Illinois

Susan Wittig Albert · Nelson Algren · Dee Brown · Iris Chang · Maxine Chernoff · David Herbert Donald · Edward Dorn · F. W. Dupee · Roger Ebert · Stanley Elkin · Jack Gelber · Paul Hoover · Stuart Kaminsky · Ron Koertge · Keith Laumer · William Maxwell · Jacquelyn Mitchard · Harry Mark Petrakis · Mary Doria Russell · Bienvenidos Santos · Robert Lewis Taylor · Mark Van Doren · Larry Woiwode

University of Iowa

Jonis Agee · R. V. Cassill · Max Allan Collins · Gayle Lynds · Merle Miller · Warren Miller · Jane Smiley · W. D. Snodgrass · Newton Thornburg · Mona Van Duyn · Tennessee Williams

University of Michigan

Max Apple · Robert L. Asprin · Sven Birkerts · Malcolm Bosse · Gillian Bradshaw · John Malcolm Brinnin · Michael Byers · Tom Clark · Max Ehrlich · Mary Gaitskill · Rhyk Gilbar · Judith Guest · Aaron Hamburger · Steve Hamilton · Jamie Harrison · Robert Hayden · Sue Hubbell · Jane Kenyon · Jane Langton · Rattawut Lapcharoensap · Melvin J. Lasky · Ross Macdonald · Mazry Mackey · Brad Meltzer · Jeffrey Meyers · Arthur Miller · Howard

Moss · Marcia Muller · Susan Orlean · Gustavo Pérez-Firmat · Marge Piercy · Ruth Reichl · William Shawn · Betty Smith · Christopher Stashoff · Glendon Swarthout · Melanie Rae Thon · Chris Van Allsburg · Henry Van Dyke · Mildred Walker · Gloria Whelan · Edmund White · Nancy Willard · Maritta Wolff

UNIVERSITY OF MINNESOTA

Poul Anderson · Elizabeth Berg · Carol Bly · Marchette Chute · Gordon Dickson · Patricia Hampl · Mark Harris · Tom Kakonis · Garrison Keillor · Lorna Landvik · Ralph McInerny · Kate Millett · Robert M. Pirsig · Kay Nolte Smith · Gerald Vizenor

UNIVERSITY OF WISCONSIN

Stephen Ambrose · Kevin J. Anderson · Charlotte Armstrong · Avi · Bill Ballinger · Saul Bellow · Paul Blackburn · Norman O. Brown · August Derleth · Kenneth Fearing · Zona Gale · Richard Gilman · Jeff Greenfield · Emily Hahn · Lorraine Hansberry · Edwin Honig · bell hooks · Hubert Kubly · Anna Lauterbach · John Muir · Joyce Carol Oates · Lance Olson · Sigurd Olson · Kenneth Patchen · Carl Rakosi · Marjorie Kinnan Rawlings · Richard Schickel · Mark Schorer · Clifford D. Simak · Scott Spencer · William Stafford · Peter Straub · Jean Toomer · Frederick J. Turner · Charlette Zolotow

---

□ LIFETIME ACHIEVEMENT AWARDS FROM THE NATIVE WRITERS' CIRCLE OF THE AMERICAS

These awards are based upon a writer's complete work to date. They are decided by a vote of members of the Native Writers' Circle of the Americas. It is the only literature prize bestowed on Indian writers by Indian people.

Paula Gunn Allen · Joseph Bruchac · Vine Deloria, Jr. · Louise Erdrich · Lee Francis III · Joy Harjo · Geary Hobson · Linda Hogan · Maurice Kenny · N. Scott Momaday · Simon J. Ortiz · Carter Revard · Leslie Marmon Silko · Gerald Vizenor · James Welch

☐ SOME SAN FRANCISCO STATE GRADUATES

Po Bronson · Ed Bullins · Tim Cahill · Don Carpenter · Carol Muske Dukes · Ernest J. Gaines · Susan Griffin · Amy Hempel · Michael McClure · Frances Mayes · Janice Mirikitani · Anne Rice · Floyd Salas · Thomas Sanchez · John Saul · Gary Soto · Gail Tsukiyama · Chelsea Quinn Yarbro

---

☐ SOME WRITERS WHO WENT TO UC BERKELEY

Susan Wittig Albert · Francesca Lia Block · Anthony Boucher · Marion Zimmer Bradley · Kate Braverman · Kim Chernin · Tony Cohan · Lucha Corpi · Edward Dahlberg · Mark Z. Danielewski · Sara Davidson · Philip K. Dick · Joan Didion · Chitra Divakaruni · Robert Duncan · Alan Dean Foster · Karen Jay Fowler · John Kenneth Galbraith · Molly Giles · Ron Goulart · Janice Gould · Edith Grossman · Barbara Guest · Oakley Hall · Diane Johnson · Pauline Kael · Alice Kaplan · Maxine Hong Kingston · John Leonard · John T. Lescroart · Leon Litwack · Ron Loewinsohn · Jack London · Terry McMillan · Greil Marcus · Josephine Miles · Valerie Miner · Craig Nova · Frank Norris · Wendy Rose · Orville Schell · Deborah Tannen · Robert K. Tannenbaum · Yoshiko Uchida · José Antonio Villarreal · Diane Wakoski

---

☐ SOME DOROTHY PARKER QUOTES

All I need is room enough to lay a hat and a few friends.

Do me a favor. When you get home, throw your mother a bone.

He [Robert Benchley] and I had an office so tiny that an inch smaller and it would have been adultery.

I require only three things of a man. He must be handsome, ruthless and stupid.

I'd rather have a bottle in front of me than a frontal lobotomy.

It serves me right for keeping all my eggs in one bastard.

Stop looking at the world through rose-colored bifocals.

If you want to know what God thought of money, just look at the people he gave it to.

The woman speaks eighteen languages, and can't say "No" in any of them.

The transatlantic crossing was so rough the only thing that I could keep on my stomach was the first mate.

□ FIRST AUTHOR TO USE TYPEWRITER

Mark Twain was the first person to submit a novel in typed form to the publisher.

□ LITTLE, BROWN & CO.

This Boston firm, founded by James Brown (died 1855) and Charles Little (died 1869), and James's son, James P. Brown, began as a publisher of law books. By 1865 it was the world's largest producer of books and texts on the law. Little, Brown's stable of writers included A. J. Cronin, Walter D. Edmonds, James Hilton, Charles Nordhoff & James Norman Hall, Edwin O'Connor, Erich Maria Remarque, and Mari Sandoz.

□ THE KORET JEWISH BOOK AWARDS (FICTION)

Sponsored by the San Francisco-based Koret Foundation in cooperation with the National Foundation for Jewish Culture, the Korets were first awarded in 1999. The winners to date:

2005 Amos Oz, *A Tale of Love and Darkness*
2004 Tony Eprile, *The Persistence of Memory*
2003 (tie) Barbara Honigmann, *A Love Made Out of Nothing & Zohara's Journey*, and Aharon Megged, *Foiglman*
2002 *The Complete Works of Isaac Babel*
2001 Philip Roth, *The Human Stain*
2000 Andre Bernard, *A Journey to the End of the Millennium: A Novel of the Middle Ages*
1999 (tie) Yoel Hoffmann, *Katschen & the Book of Joseph*, and Brian Morton, *Starting Out in the Evening*

☐ GREAT MODERN JEWISH AMERICAN FICTION

The 100 Greatest Works of Modern Jewish Literature compiled by the National Yiddish Book Center includes these English language novels and short-story collections by American authors:

Saul Bellow, *Herzog* (1964) and
Mr. Sammler's Planet (1970)
Abraham Cahan, *The Rise of David Levinsky* (1917)
Michael Chabon, *The Amazing Adventures of Kavalier & Clay* (2000)
Daniel Fuchs, *The Williamsburg Trilogy* (1961)
Bernard Malamud, *The Complete Stories* (1997)
Cynthia Ozick, *The Pagan Rabbi* (1971)
Henry Roth, *Call It Sleep* (1934)
Delmore Schwartz, *In Dreams Begin Responsibilities* (1938)
Milton Steinberg, *As a Driven Leaf* (1939)

☐ MULTIPLE WINNERS OF NATIONAL JEWISH BOOK AWARD (FICTION)

Chaim Grade · Johanna Kaplan · Cynthia Ozick · Philip Roth · A. B. Yehoshua

---

☐ SOME FORMER TEXAS STUDENTS

Baylor

Thomas Harris · Allan Weir

North Texas State

Bill Brammer · John Jerome · Grover Lewis · Larry McMurtry

Rice

Catherine Savage Brosman · John Graves · William Goyen · Elizabeth Moon

Southern Methodist

Beth Henley · William Humphrey · John J. Nance · Terry Southern

Texas Christian

Sandra Benitez · Sandra Brown · William Harrison · Sue Monk Kidd

University of Houston

Donald Barthelme · Vikram Chandra · Padgett Powell

University of Texas

Steve Barthelme · John Canaday · Benjamin Capps · J. M. Coetzee · Catherine Coulter · Bill Crider · Kinky Friedman · Shelby Hearon · Rolando Hinojosa · Elmer Kelton · Joe Lansdale · Colum McCann · Willie Morris · Stephen Oates · Sharon Kay Penman · Rick Riordan · James Sallis · Steven Saylor · Sandra Scofield · Bruce Sterling · Whitley Strieber

---

□ YOUNGEST PULITZER PRIZE WINNER (FICTION)

Jhumpa Lahiri was thirty-two in 2000 when she was awarded a Pulitzer Prize for her short story collection, *Interpreter of Maladies.*

□ PEN/FAULKNER AWARD FOR FICTION

This $15,000 prize is given each year for the best work of fiction by an American author.

2005 Ha Jin, *War Trash*
2004 John Updike, *The Early Stories*
2003 Sabina Murray, *The Caprices*
2002 Ann Patchett, *Bel Canto*
2001 Philip Roth, *The Human Stain*
2000 Ha Jin, *Waiting*
1999 Michael Cunningham, *The Hours*
1998 Rafi Zabor, *The Bear Comes Home*
1997 Gina Berriault, *Women in Their Beds*
1996 Richard Ford, *Independence Day*
1995 David Guterson, *Snow Falling on Cedars*

1994 Philip Roth, *Operation Shylock*
1993 E. Annie Proulx, *Postcards*
1992 Don DeLillo, *Mao II*
1991 John Edgar Wideman, *Philadelphia Fire*
1990 E. L. Doctorow, *Billy Bathgate*
1989 James Salter, *Dusk*
1988 T. Coraghessan Boyle, *World's End*
1987 Richard Wiley, *Soldiers in Hiding*
1986 Peter Taylor, *The Old Forest*
1985 Tobias Wolff, *The Barracks Thief*
1984 John Edgar Wideman, *Sent for You Yesterday*
1983 Toby Olson, *Seaview*
1982 David Bradley, *The Chaneyville Incident*
1981 Walter Abish, *How German Is It*

☐ SOME WRITERS EDITED BY GARY FISKETJON

An editor-at-large at Knopf, Fisketjon joined Random House in 1978, was responsible for launching the popular Vintage Contemporaries series in 1984, and has edited such distinguished writers as:

Julian Barnes · Peter Carey · Raymond Carver · Annie Dillard · Brett Easton Ellis · Richard Ford · Kent Haruf · Cormac McCarthy · Jay McInerny · Haruki Murakami · Richard Russo · Graham Swift · Donna Tartt · Joy Williams · Tobias Wolff

---

☐ SIMON & SCHUSTER

Founded in 1924 by Richard L. Simon and M. Lincoln Schuster. Their first project was a crossword puzzle book, the first ever published, which was a huge bestseller. Over time the company grew to be one of the largest publishers in the United States. It has won fifty-four Pulitzer Prizes and been the recipient of numerous National Book Awards and National Book Critics Circle Awards.

☐ NATIONAL BOOK AWARD WINNERS

Since 1950 the National Book Foundation has bestowed each an annual award for the best books by American authors. Winners for the twenty-first century in fiction and nonfiction are:

Fiction	General Nonfiction
2004 *The News from Paraguay* by Lily Tuck	*Arc of Justice: A Saga of Race, Civil Rights and Murder in the Jazz Age* by Kevin Boyle
2003 *The Great Fire* by Shirley Hazzard	*Waiting for Snow in Havana: Confessions of a Cuban Boy* by Carlos Eire
2002 *Three Junes* by Julia Glass	*Master of the Senate: The Years of Lyndon Johnson* by Robert Caro
2001 *The Corrections* by Jonathan Franzen	*The Noonday Demon: An Atlas of Depression* by Andrew Solomon
2000 *In America* by Susan Sontag	*In the Heart of the Sea: The Tragedy of the Whaleship Essex* by Nathaniel Philbrick

---

☐ LANNAN LIFETIME ACHIEVEMENT AWARD WINNERS

The following writers have received the Lannan Foundation's lifetime achievement award of $200,000:

John Barth · John Berger · Kay Boyle · Evan S. Connell · Robert Creeley · William Gaddis · William H. Gass · Peter Matthiessen · W. S. Merwin · Adrienne Rich · Edward Said · R. S. Thomas

☐ SOME FORMER UNIVERSITY OF MISSOURI STUDENTS

Win Blevins · Jerry Bumpus · James Lee Burke · Craig Claiborne · Glen Cook · Deborah Digges · Philip Jose Farmer · Charles G. Finney · Bruce Jay Friedman · Barry Gifford · Diane Glancy · Dorothy B. Hughes · Haynes Johnson · Jonathan Kwitney · Jim Lehrer · Richard Matheson · Marijane Meaker · William Least Heat-Moon · Eric Pankey · Nancy Pickard · Berton Roueche · Bob Shacochis · Luke Short · Roger Straus · Margaret Weis · Tennessee Williams · Lanford Wilson

---

☐ A FEW FORMER UNIVERSITY OF NEBRASKA STUDENTS

Ted Kooser · Patricia McGerr · Mari Sandoz · Jim Thompson

☐ SOME WRITERS WHO WENT TO THE UNIVERSITY OF KANSAS

Evan S. Connell, Jr. · Connie May Fowler · James E. Gunn · Frank Harris · William Inge · Antonya Nelson · Sara Paretsky · Ridley Pearson · Rex Stout · Daniel Woodrell

---

☐ MULTIPLE WINNERS OF THE GOLDEN SPUR

Since 1954 the Western Writers of America has presented its Golden Spur Award for, among others, the best traditional Western novel. In all those years only six authors have won it more than once:

Benjamin Capps · Robert J. Conley · Fred Grove · Douglas C. Jones · Elmer Kelton · Richard S. Wheeler

---

☐ FIRST WESTERN

The first novel in English set in the West was Timothy Flint's *Francis Berrian, or the Mexican Patriot* (1826).

☐ W. W. NORTON & COMPANY

W. W. Norton & Company, the oldest and largest publishing house owned wholly by its employees, dates back to 1923 when William Warder Norton and Margaret D. Herter Norton began publishing lectures delivered at the People's Institute, the adult education division of New York City's Cooper Union. Authors include Andrea Barrett, Jared Diamond, Sigmund Freud, Stephen Jay Gould, Seamus Heaney, Patricia Highsmith, Patrick O'Brien, Adrienne Rich, and Irvine Welsh.

☐ JASON EPSTEIN

Longtime editorial director of Random House, generally credited with launching the "paperback revolution" when he established the trade paperback format in 1952, he founded the *New York Review of Books* and the Library of America. Writers whom he edited include E. L. Doctorow, Norman Mailer, Vladimir Nabokov, Philip Roth, and Gore Vidal.

☐ SOME FORMER UCLA STUDENTS

Dorothy Baker · Lois Battle · Nash Candelaria · Anne Edwards · Steve Erickson · Faye Kellerman · Jonathan Kellerman · Katherine Kurtz · Russell Leong · Jack Ludwig · Steve Martin · Deena Metzger · Josephine Miles · Gina Nahai · Mary Helen Ponce · Nancy Taylor Rosenberg · Geoff Ryman · Oliver Sacks · Greg Sarris · Carolyn See · Harry Turtledove

---

☐ SOME UC-IRVINE CREATIVE WRITING MFAS (FICTION)

Aimee Bender · Michael Chabon · Leonard Chang · Jill Ciment · Richard Ford · Glen David Gold · Jay Gummerman · Louis B. Jones · Marti Leimbach · Maile Meloy · Kem Nunn · Whitney Otto · Alice Sebold · Roberta Smoodin · Katherine Vaz · Helena María Viramontes

☐ SOME UNIVERSITY OF NEW MEXICO ALUMNI

Rudolfo Anaya · Denise Chavez · Joy Harjo · Tony Hillerman · N. Scott Momaday · Simon J. Ortiz · Leslie Marmon Silko

---

☐ A FEW FORMER UNIVERSITY OF OKLAHOMA STUDENTS

Gregory Benford · Bill Gulick · Fred Harris · Carolyn G. Hart · Tony Hillerman · Judson Jerome · Azar Nafisi · Tim Sandlin · Ross Thomas

---

☐ SOME FORMER UNIVERSITY OF WASHINGTON STUDENTS

Tim Cahill · Robert Cantwell · Bev Cleary · Ivan Doig · David Eddings · Carrolly Erickson · G. M. Ford · Debora Greger · David Guterson · Frank Herbert · Thom Jones · Jerry Pournelle · Tom Robbins · Marilynne Robinson · Ann Rule · Megan Terry · James A. Wright

---

☐ SOME TOM ROBBINS QUOTES

A sense of humor, properly developed, is superior to any religion so far devised.

Birth and death were easy. It was life that was hard.

Politics is for people who have a passion for changing life but lack a passion for living it.

It's never too late to have a happy childhood.

Using words to describe magic is like using a screwdriver to cut roast beef.

Of the seven dwarves, only Dopey had a shaven face. This should tell you something about the custom of shaving.

The beauty of simplicity is the complexity it attracts.

We waste time looking for the perfect lover instead of creating the perfect love.

If little else the brain is an educational toy.

We're our own dragons as well as our own heroes, and we have to rescue ourselves from ourselves.

Humanity has advanced, when it has advanced, not because it has been sober, responsible, and cautious, but because it has been playful, rebellious, and immature.

Disbelief in magic can force a poor soul into believing in government and business.

Love is the ultimate outlaw. It just won't adhere to any rules. The most any of us can do is sign on as its accomplice. Instead of vowing to honor and obey, maybe we should swear to aid and abet.

To achieve the impossible, it is precisely the unthinkable that must be thought.

We, with our propensity for murder, torture, slavery, rape, cannibalism, pillage, advertising jingles, shag carpets, and golf, how could we seriously be considered as the perfection of a four-billion-year-old grandiose experiment?

You don't have to be a genius to recognize one. If you did, Einstein would never have gotten invited to the White House.

There are many things worth living for, there are a few things worth dying for, but there's nothing worth killing for.

□ CHARLES SCRIBNER

In 1846, Charles Scribner (1821-1871) founded the publishing firm that would become Charles Scribner's Sons and would publish such authors as Henry Adams, F. Scott Fitzgerald, Ernest Hemingway, James Jones, Ring Lardner, Alan Paton, Marjorie Kinnan Rawlings, Theodore Roosevelt, Edith Wharton, and Thomas Wolfe.

☐ BEST ASIAN AMERICAN LITERATURE

Since 1998, the Annual Asian American Literary Awards have honored Asian American writers for excellence in fiction, poetry, creative nonfiction, memoir, stage plays, and screenplays.

2004 Mei-Mei Berssenbrugge, *Nest*
Monique Truong, *The Book of Salt*
Vijay Vaitheeswaran, *Power to the People*
2003 Walter Lew, *Treadwinds: Poems and Intermedia Texts*
Meera Nair, *Video: Stories*
Julie Otsuka, *When the Emperor Was Divine*
2002 Alexander Chee, *Edinburgh*
Luis H. Francia, *Eye of the Fish: A Personal Archipelago*
Christina Chiu, *Troublemaker and Other Saints*
2001 Ha Jin, *Bridegroom and Other Stories*
Eugene Gloria, *Drivers at the Short Time Motel: Poems*
Akhil Sharma, *An Obedient Father*
2000 Eric Gamalinda, *Zero Gravity*
Chang-rae Lee, *A Gesture Life*
1999 Susan Choi, *The Foreign Student*
Arthur Sze, *The Redshifting Web: Poems 1970–98*
1998 Mei-Mei Berssenbrugge, *Endocrinology*
Lois-Ann Yamanaka, *Blu's Hanging*

☐ SOME AUTODIDACTS

These American writers never went to college or dropped out after a short stint of collegiate life.

James Baldwin · R. P. Blackmur · Truman Capote · John Cheever · James Fenimore Cooper · Gregory Corso · Hart Crane · Gloria Emerson · Dashiell Hammett · Bret Harte · Ernest Hemingway · William Dean Howells · Langston Hughes · Ring Lardner · H. L. Mencken · Eugene O'Neill · Dorothy Parker · Kenneth Patchen · Dawn Powell · Kenneth Rexroth · Damon Runyon · J. D. Salinger · Carl Sandburg · William Saroyan · Hubert Selby · Upton Sinclair · Gore Vidal · Edith Wharton · Marianne Wiggins · Richard Wright

□ SOME RHODES SCHOLARS

Stringfellow Barr · James H. Billington · Daniel J. Boorstin · Cleanth Brooks · Guy Davenport · Leslie Epstein · Brian Greene · Jonathan Kozol · Thomas McGrath · Christopher Morley · Willie Morris · Reynolds Price · David Quammen · John Crowe Ransom · William Jay Smith · Robert Penn Warren · John Edgar Wideman · Naomi Wolf

---

□ SOME ENGLISH-BORN WRITERS IN AMERICA

Piers Anthony · W. H. Auden · Eric Bentley · Clive Barker · Barbara Taylor Bradford · Anne Bradstreet · Frances Hodgson Burnett · Taylor Caldwell · Lee Child · John Collier · Fred D'Aguilar · George Dangerfield · Malcolm Gladwell · Edgar Guest · Thom Gunn · Frank Harris · Aldous Huxley · Christopher Isherwood · Pico Iyer · Jhumpa Lahiri · Denise Levertov · Hugh Lofting · Jonathan Raban · Charles Sheffield · Paul West · P. G. Wodehouse

---

□ BRITISH NOBEL PRIZE WINNERS (LITERATURE)

Winston Churchill · T. S. Eliot · John Galsworthy · William Golding · Rudyard Kipling · V. S. Naipaul · Bertrand Russell · George Bernard Shaw

---

□ FIRST PRESIDENT OF PEN

The English Nobel Prize-winning novelist John Galsworthy was the first president of what would become International PEN in the early 1920s. Its aims were "to promote intellectual co-operation and understanding amongst writers; to create a world community of writers that would emphasize the central role of literature in the development of world culture; and to defend literature against the many threats to its survival which the modern world poses." PEN is an acronym for poets, playwrights, essayists, editors, and novelists.

□ RICHEST NONFICTION PRIZE

In 1999 the Samuel Johnson Prize was welcomed by a literary world in which there had been a paucity of prestigious prizes for nonfiction. Sponsored anonymously by a retired British businessman, the annual prize is worth £30,000 to the winner.

2005 *Like a Fiery Elephant: The Story of B. S. Johnson* by Jonathan Coe
2004 *Stasiland: Stories from Behind the Berlin Wall* by Anna Funder
2003 *Pushkin* by T. J. Binyon
2002 *Peacemakers Paris 1919: Six Months That Changed the World* by Margaret Macmillan
2001 *The Third Reich* by Michael Burleigh
2000 *Berlioz*, Vol. 2 by David Cairns
1999 *Stalingrad* by Antony Beever

□ SOME TITLES FROM SHAKESPEARE

Brave New World Aldous Huxley	O Brave new world That hath such people in it! – The Tempest
Bare Ruined Choirs Gary Willis	That time of year thou mayst in me behold / When yellow leaves, or none, or few, do hang / Upon those boughs which shake against the cold / Bare ruin'd choirs, where late sweet the birds sang. – Sonnet LXXIII
Nothing Like the Sun Anthony Burgess	My mistress' eyes are nothing like the sun; coral is far more red than lips are red; If snow be white, why then her breasts are dun… – Sonnet CXXX
Gaudy Night Dorothy L. Sayers	Let's have one other gaudy night. Call to me /All my sad captains; fill out bowls once more; / Let's mock the midnight bell. – Antony and Cleopatra

Something Wicked This Way Comes Ray Bradbury	By the Pricking of my thumbs Something wicked this way comes. – MACBETH
The Sound and the Fury William Faulkner	Life's . . . a tale told by an idiot, full of sound and fury, Signifying nothing. – MACBETH
The Moon Is Down John Steinbeck	The moon is down; I have not heard the clock. – MACBETH
Pale Fire Vladimir Nabokov	. . . The moon's an arrant thief and her pale fire she snatches from the sun. – TIMON OF ATHENS
In Cold Blood Truman Capote	Who cannot condemn rashness in cold blood? – TIMON OF ATHENS
The Darling Buds of May H. E. Bates	Rough winds do shake the darling buds of May / And summer's lease hath all too short a date. – Sonnet XVIII
Cold Comfort Farm Stella Gibbons	I do not ask you much: I beg cold comfort. – KING JOHN
Cakes and Ale W. Somerset Maugham	Dost thou think, because thou art virtuous, there shall be no more cakes and ale? – TWELFTH NIGHT
The Mousetrap Agatha Christie	KING: What do you call the play? HAMLET: The Mouse-trap. Marry, how? Tropically. This play is the image of a murder done in Vienna. – HAMLET
Remembrance of Things Past Marcel Proust (Moncrieff, trans.)	When to the sessions of sweet silent thought / I summon up remembrance of things past, / I sigh the lack of many a thing I sought. . . – Sonnet XXX
The Dogs of War Frederick Forsyth	Cry "Havoc!" and let slip the dogs of war. – JULIUS CAESAR

☐ A FEW AUTHORS WHO RENOUNCED U.S. CITIZENSHIP

W. E. B. Du Bois · T. S. Eliot · Henry James

☐ SOME CHARACTER NAMES FROM DICKENS

Tite Barnacle · Noddy Boffin · Serjeant Buzfuz · Mercy Pecksniff · Ninette Crummles Trabb · Frederic Verisopht · Volumnea Dedlock · Affery Flintwinc · Lucretia Tox · Wopsie · Wackford Squeers · Prince Turveydrop · Rogue Riderhood · Durdles Creakle · Cheggs Pumblechook · M'Choakumchild · Fezziwig · Jellyby Vholes Wardle

---

☐ MAXIMS OF GEORGE BERNARD SHAW

If you cannot get rid of the family skeleton, you may as well make it dance.

Lack of money is the root of all evil.

The fact that a believer is happier than a skeptic is no more to the point than a drunken man is happier than a sober one.

Martyrdom is the only way in which a man can become famous without ability.

Do you know what a pessimist is? A man who thinks everybody is as nasty as himself, and hates them for it.

There are two tragedies in life. One is not to get your heart's desire. The other is to get it.

Parentage is a very important profession, but no test of fitness for it is ever imposed in the interest of children.

He knows nothing, and he thinks he knows nearly everything. That points to a political career.

The golden rule is that there are no golden rules.

Hegel was right when he said that we learn from history that man can never learn anything from history

A fashion is nothing but an induced epidemic.

GEORGE BERNARD SHAW

A perpetual holiday is a working definition of hell.

Youth is a wonderful thing. What a crime to waste it on children.

Democracy is a device that ensures that we shall be governed no better than we deserve.

The worst sin toward our fellow creatures is not to hate them, but to be indifferent to them; that's the essence of inhumanity.

I often quote myself. It adds spice to my conversation.

Liberty means responsibility. That is why most men dread it.

He who has never hoped can never despair.

Reading made Don Quixote a gentleman. Believing what he read made him mad.

Silence is the most perfect expression of scorn.

□ SOME BRITISH PEN NAMES

George Bourne (George Sturt)
Anthony Burgess (John Burgess Wilson)
Lewis Carroll (Charles Lutwidge Dodgson)
Lord Dunsany (Edward Plunkett)
George Eliot (Mary Ann Evans)
Nicci French (Nicci Gerard & Sean French)
Lewis Grassic Gibbon (James Leslie Mitchell)
Henry Green (Henry Yorke)
James Herriot (James Wright)
Sophie Kinsella (Madeleine Wickham)
John Le Carré (David Cornwall)
Hugh MacDiarmid (Christopher Grieve)
Katharine Mansfield (Kathleen Beauchamp)
Flann O'Brien (Brian Nolan)
Frank O'Connor (Michael O'Donovan)
George Orwell (Eric Blair)
Ouida (Marie Louise de la Ramée)
Miss Read (Doris Jessie Saint)
Mary Renault (Mary Challans)
Saxe Rohmer (Arthur Sarsfield Ward)

Mark Rutherford (William Hale White)
Nevil Shute (Nevil Norway)
Saki (H. H. Munro)
William Trevor (William Cox)
Mrs. Humphrey Ward (Mary Augusta Arnold)
Rebecca West (Cecily Andrews)

□ SOME BRITISH AUTHORS DEAD IN THEIR THRITIES

Emily Brontë (30) · Charlotte Brontë (39) · Robert Burns (37) · Lord Byron (36) · Ernest Dowson (33) · Richard Jefferies (38) · Katharine Mansfield (35) · Joe Orton (34) · Robert Southwell (34) · Dylan Thomas (37) · Edward Thomas (39) · Thomas Traherne (37) · Denton Welch (33) · John Wilmot (33) · Thomas Wyatt (39)

□ BRITISH AUTHORS PRONUNCIATION GUIDE

W. H. Auden: AWED-in
Alan Ayckbourn: AKE-born
Samuel Taylor Coleridge: KOHL-rij
Abraham Cowley: COOL-ee
William Cowper: KOO-per
Roald Dahl: ROO-ul Doll
Charles L. Dodgson: DAHD-sun
Louis de Berniers: Loo-EE duh BAIRN-yair
Alain de Boton: ah-LAN duh bo-TOHN
John Donne: DUHN
Lawrence Durrell: DUR-ul (as in "girl")
Eva Figes: FIE-jess
Edmund Gosse: GAWS
Seamus Heaney: HEE-nee
Aldous Huxley: AWL-duhs
John Le Carré: Luh-car-RAY
Anthony Powell: ANT-ony PO-ell (as in Lowell)
Jean Rhys: RICE
Lytton Strachey: LIT-ahn STRAY-chih

John Millington Synge: SING
William Makepeace Thackeray: THACK-ree
Colin Thubron: THOO-bron
Colm Toíbin: toe-BEEN
J. R. R. Tolkien: tohl-KEEN
Evelyn Waugh: EEV-lin WAH
P. G. Wodehouse: WUD-hows
Mary Wollstonecraft: WEUL-stuhn-kraft
William B. Yeats: YAYTS

□ MOST ENJOYABLE BRITISH BOOKS

The Whitbread Book Awards (est. 1971) aim to celebrate the most enjoyable British writing of the past year, regardless of category. The winner of the Book of the Year Award receives £30,000. Recent winners include:

2004 *Small Island*, by Andrea Levy
2003 *The Curious Incident of the Dog in the Night-Time* by Mark Haddon
2002 *Samuel Pepys: The Unequalled Self* by Claire Tomalin
2001 *The Amber Spyglass* by Philip Pullman
2000 *English Passengers* by Matthew Kneale
1999 *Beowulf* translated by Seamus Heaney
1998 *Birthday Letters* by Ted Hughes
1997 *Tales from Ovid* by Ted Hughes
1996 *The Spirit Level* by Seamus Heaney
1995 *Behind the Scenes at the Museum* by Kate Atkinson
1994 *Felicia's Journey* by William Trevor
1993 *The Theory of War* by Joan Brady
1992 *Swing Hammer Swing!* by Jeff Torrington
1991 *A Life of Picasso* by John Richardson
1990 *Hopeful Monsters* by Nicholas Mosley

□ MOST PROLIFIC WRITER OF ROMANCE FICTION

Barbara Cartland, with more than 600 million copies of her books in print.

☐ SOME FORMER ENGLISH POETS LAUREATE

John Betjeman · Robert Bridges · Cecil Day-Lewis · John Dryden · Ted Hughes · John Masefield · Robert Southey · Alfred Lord Tennyson · William Wordsworth

---

☐ TWENTY-FIRST-CENTURY BOOKER PRIZE WINNERS

England's most prestigious award for fiction is the Man Booker Prize. The winners since 2000 are:

2004 *The Line of Beauty* by Alan Hollinghurst
2003 *Vernon God Little* by D. B. C. Pierre
2002 *Life of Pi* by Yann Martel
2001 *The True History of the Kelly Gang* by Peter Carey
2000 *The Blind Assassin* by Margaret Atwood

☐ SOME WRITERS EDITED BY DIANA ATHILL

Diana Athill (b. 1919) spent fifty years as an editor, most of them at London's André Deutsch Limited. The many writers she worked with include:

Molly Keane · Jack Kerouac · Brian Moore · V. S. Naipaul · George Orwell · Jean Rhys · Mordecai Richler · Philip Roth · John Updike

---

☐ SOME CLICHÉS FROM ENGLISH LITERATURE

Barkis is willin': Charles Dickens, *David Copperfield*
Bloody but unbowed: W. E. Henley, *Invictus*
Butter wouldn't melt in her mouth: Charles Macklin, *The Man of the World*
Captain of one's soul: W. E. Henley, *Invictus*
Cynosure of all eyes: John Milton, *L'Allegro*
Damn with faint praise: Alexander Pope, *Prologue to the Satires*
Each man kills the thing he loves: Oscar Wilde, *The Ballad of Reading Gaol*

East is East and West is West is West: Rudyard Kipling, *The Ballad of East and West*
Far from the madding crowd: Thomas Gray, *Elegy Written in a Country Churchyard*
I am monarch of all I survey: William Cowper, *Truth* (atttributed to Alexander Selkirk)
Sadder and a wiser man: Samuel Taylor Coleridge, *The Rime of the Ancient Mariner*
Slough of despond: John Bunyan, *Pilgrim's Progress*
Speed the parting guest: Homer, *Odyssey* (Pope's translation)
Sweetness and light: Jonathan Swift, *The Battle of the Books*
Swim into one's ken: John Keats, *On First Looking into Chapman's Homer*
The law is an ass: Dickens, *Oliver Twist*
'Tis better to have loved and lost than never to have loved at all: Alfred Lord Tennyson, *In Memoriam*
Truth is beauty, beauty truth: Keats, *Ode on a Grecian Urn*
Water, water everywhere, nor any drop to drink: Coleridge, *The Rime of the Ancient Mariner*

☐ SOME WELL-WORN PHRASES FROM SHAKESPEARE

A charmed Life (*Macbeth*)
Chronicle small beer (*Othello*)
Dance attendance on (*Henry VIII*)
A Daniel come to judgment (*The Merchant of Venice*)
Every inch a king (*King Lear*)
The green-eyed monster (*Othello*)
Lay it on with a trowel (*As You Like It*)
More honored in the breach than the observance (*Hamlet*)
More in sorrow than in anger (*Hamlet*)
More sinned against than sinning (*King Lear*)
Murder most foul (*Hamlet*)
Lay on, Macduff (*Macbeth*)
Lean and hungry look (*Julius Caesar*)
Slings and arrows of outrageous fortune (*Hamlet*)
To smell to Heaven (*Hamlet*)

Such stuff are dreams made on (*Hamlet*)
That way madness lies (*King Lear*)
To the manner born (*Hamlet*)
The unkindest cut of all (*Julius Caesar*)
We shall not look upon his like again (*Hamlet*)
To wear one's heart on one's sleeve (*Othello*)
The world's a stage (*As You Like It*)
The world's mine oyster (*The Merry Wives of Windsor*)

☐ A FEW TITLES FROM MILTON

In Dubious Battle (John Steinbeck): *Paradise Lost*
Eyeless in Gaza (Aldous Huxley): "Samson Agonistes"
Precious Bane (Mary Webb): *Paradise Lost*
Look Homeward, Angel (Thomas Wolfe): "Lycidas"
The Cricket on the Hearth (Charles Dickens): "Il Penseroso"

☐ SOME EUROPEAN-BORN WRITERS IN AMERICA

Walter Abish (Germany) · Louis Agassiz (Switzerland) · Vassily Aksyonov (Russia) · Martha Albrand (Germany) · Sholem Aleichim (Ukraine) · Hannah Arendt (Germany) · Sholem Asch (Poland) · Isaac Asimov (Russia) · Jacques Barzun (France) · Vicki Baum (Austria) · Louis Begley (Poland) · Ludwig Bemelmans (Austria) · Bernard Berenson (Lithuania) · Maeve Brennan (Ireland) · Hermann Broch (Germany) · Joseph Brodsky (Russia) · Charles Bukowski (Germany) · Abraham Cahan (Russia) · Paul de Man (Belgium) · René Dubos (France) · Joe Esterhaz (Hungary) · Nicholas Gage (Greece) · Francine du Plessix Gray (France) · Lucy Grealy (Ireland) · Eamon Grennan (Ireland) · Jorge Guillen (Spain) · Geoffrey H. Hartman (Germany) · Ursula Hegi (Germany) · Alexander Hemon (Bosnia) · Hans Koning (Netherlands) · Jerzy Kosinski (Poland) · Walter Laquer (Germany) · Gerda Lerner (Austria) · Ludwig Lewisohn (Germany) · John Lukacs (Hungary) · Janet Malcolm (Czechoslovakia) · Norman Manea (Romania) · Malachi Martin (Ireland) · Colum McCann (Ireland) · Frank McCourt (Ireland) · Herbert

Marcuse (Germany) · Lisel Mueller (Germany) · Paul Muldoon (Ireland) · Josip Novakovich (Yugoslavia) · Erwin Panofsky (Germany) Ernst Pawel (Germany) · Otto Penzler (Germany) · Ayn Rand (Russia) · Philip Rahv (Russia) · Mayne Reid (Ireland) · Henry Roth (Ukraine) · May Sarton (Belgium) · Lore Segal (Austria) · Charles Simic (Yugoslavia) · Isaac Bashevis Singer (Poland) · Curt Siodmak (Germany) · Gary Shteyngart (Russia) · George Steiner (France) Tad Szulc (Poland) · Lara Vapmyar (Russia) · Janwillem van de Wetrering (Netherlands) · Marguerite Yourcenar (France) · Anzia Yezierska (Poland)

□ SOME EUROPEAN WRITERS WHO DIED IN THEIR THIRTIES

Catullus (30) · Jaroslav Hasek (39) · Jens Peter Jacobsen (38) · Alfred Jarry (34) · Giacomo Leopardi (39) · Federico García Lorca (38) · Vladimir Mayakovsky (37) · Henry Murger (39) · Irene Nemirovsky (39) · Aleksandr Pushkin (38) · Arthur Rimbaud (37) · J. M. Synge (38) · Boris Vian (39)

□ THE GREAT LIBRARIES OF THE ANCIENT WORLD

1. The library of King Ashurbanipal, in Nineveh. Considered "the first systematically collected library", it was rediscovered in the nineteenth century.

2. The Royal Library of Alexandria, once the largest in the world, founded by Ptolemy II of Egypt in the third century B.C.

3. The Villa of the Papyri, in Herculaneum. One of the largest libraries of ancient Rome. Thought to have been destroyed in the eruption of Mount Vesuvius. Rediscovered in 1752.

4. At Pergamum the Attalid kings formed the second best classical library after Alexandria, founded in emulation of the Ptolemies.

5. Cæsarea Palæstina had a great early Christian library. Through Origen and the scholarly priest Pamphilus, the theo-

logical school of Cæsarea won a reputation for having the most extensive ecclesiastical library of the time, containing more than 30,000 manuscripts.

☐ SOME LATIN EXPRESSIONS EVERY READER SHOULD KNOW

AD ABSURDUM: To the point of absurdity.

AD HOMINEM: "To the man," appealing to prejudice.

AD INFINITUM: Endlessly.

AD NAUSEAM: To the point of making one sick.

ANTEBELLUM: Belonging to period before the Civil War.

CARPE DIEM: "Seize the day."

CUM: With.

DEUS EX MACHINA: An improbable plot device used by author to work his/her way out of a difficult situation.

DRAMATIS PERSONÆ: The characters of a play.

EX LIBRIS: From the books (of).

FINIS: The end.

IN FLAGRANTE DELICTO: In the act of committing a crime.

IN MEDIA RES: "In the midst of things"; opening story in the middle of the action.

IN SITU: In position.

IN TOTO: Completely.

INCUNABULUM: Book printed before 1501.

INDEX LIBRUM PROHIBITORUM: List of forbidden books.

JUVENILIA: Works produced in youth.

LITERATI: Men and women of letters.

MAGNUM OPUS: Great work, masterpiece.

MEA CULPA: My fault.

MISCELLANEA: Collection of varied written items.

MODUS VIVENDI: Way of living.

HOMER

NON SEQUITUR: It does not follow.

OBITER DICTA: Incidental remark.

OMNIUM GATHERUM: Miscellaneous collection.

PACE: With all due respect or apologies.

PASSIM: All through.

RARA AVIS: Rare bird.

SIC: Thus or so (usually in brackets when inserted in a quoted passage).

TABULA RASA: Blank slate.

VADE MECUM: Handbook.

VERBATIM: Word for word.

☐ SOURCES OF SOME EPONYMS FROM CLASSIC LITERATURE

ACHILLES' HEEL: In Greek mythology, the protagonist in Homer's *The Iliad.*

ARISTOTELEAN: From Aristotle.

CASSANDRA: In Greek mythology, appears in works of Aeschylus, Euripides, and Virgil.

CLOUD CUCKOO LAND: From Aristophanes, *The Birds.*

ELECTRA COMPLEX: In Greek legend, appears in plays by Aeschylus, Euripides, and Sophocles.

HOMERIC: From Homer.

OEDIPUS COMPLEX: In Greek mythology, subject of two plays by Sophocles.

PLATONIC LOVE: From Plato.

SOCRATIC METHOD: Socrates, from works of Plato.

TROJAN HORSE: From Virgil's *Aeneid.*

☐ DERIVATION OF "ANTHOLOGY"

The word for a collection of literary pieces literally means in Greek "flower gathering." Originally a collection of "flowers of literature," that is, beautiful passages from authors, especially a "bouquet" of Greek epigrams.

☐ ORIGIN OF "CLASSIC"

Servius divided the Romans into five classes. A citizen of the highest class was called *classicus.* The rest were said to be *infra classem,* that is, beneath the class. Accordingly, authors of the best or first class were termed *classici auctores* ("classic authors"). The term has come to describe any work of the first or highest order and of enduring value.

☐ SOME USEFUL LATIN ABBREVIATIONS

CA. or *C.* (*circa*): About. Used before approximate dates of figures.

CF. (*confer*): Compare (one thing with another).

ET AL. (*et alia, et alii*): And other(s).

ETC. (*et cetera*): And so on.

E.G. (*exempli gratis*): For example.

IBID. (*ibidem*): In the same place.

I.E. (*id est*): That is.

LOC. CIT. (*loco citato*): In the place cited.

N.B. (*nota bene*): "Note well."

OP. CIT. (*opere citato*): In the work cited.

Q. E. D.: (*quod erat demonstrandum*): Which was to be proved.

Q.V. (*quod vide*): Which see, see this thing.

VIZ. (*vidilicet*): Namely.

☐ FRENCH NOBEL PRIZE WINNERS (LITERATURE)

Henri Bergson · Albert Camus · Roger Martin du Gard · Anatole France · François Mauriac · Frédéric Mistral · Saint-John Perse · Sully Prudhomme · Romain Rolland · Jean Paul Sartre · Claude Simon

□ FIRST AMERICAN ELECTED TO THE ACADÉMIE FRANÇAISE

The first person of American parentage to be elected to the Académie Française was Julien Green (1900–1998), who was elected in 1971, a year after winning the academy's grand prize for literature.

□ FRENCH AUTHORS PRONUNCIATION GUIDE

Jean Anouilh: ah-NOO
Antonin Artaud: AN-to-nan art-OH
Guillaume Apollinaire: gee-YOME ah-paw-lee-NER
Roland Barthes: Ro-LAN bahrt
Pierre Corneille: kawr-NAY
Gustave Flaubert: floh-BER
Stéphane Mallarmé: STAY-fan mal-lahr-MAY
Marcel Proust: PROOST
Arthur Rimbaud: RAM-boh
Alain Robbe-Grillet: ah-LAN rob-gree-YAY
Nathalie Sarraute: nah-to-LEE sah-ROTE

□ SOME MOLIÈRE QUOTES

I assure you that a learned fool is more foolish than an ignorant fool.

I prefer an accommodating vice to an obstinate virtue.

Nearly all men die of their remedies, and not of their illnesses.

Of all follies there is none greater than wanting to make the world a better place.

We die only once, and for such a long time.

Of all the noises known to man, opera is the most expensive.

Writing is like prostitution. First you do it for love, and then for a few close friends, and then for money.

☐ THE GREATEST FRENCH NOVELS

In 2003 The Observer *of London put forth its list of the one hundred greatest novels of all time. It included the following French novels:*

The Black Sheep by Honoré de Balzac
The Charterhouse of Parma by Stendhal
The Count of Monte Cristo by Alexandre Dumas fils
Dangerous Liaisons by Pierre Choderlos de Laclos
In Search of Lost Time by Marcel Proust
Journey to the End of the Night by Louis-Ferdinand Céline
The Plague by Albert Camus

☐ SOME FRENCH EVERY READER SHOULD KNOW

APERÇU: A brief sketch.

AVANT-GARDE: A group operating in advance of the main body.

ARRIVISTE: A social climber.

BELLES LETTRES: "Beautiful writing," literature.

BÊTE NOIRE: "Black beast," a bugbear.

BIBELOT: A trinket.

BON MOT: A witty remark.

CHEF-D'ŒUVRE: A masterpiece.

CONTE: A short tale.

COTERIE: A small group of persons who associate frequently.

DEMIMONDE: "Half-world," a social group existing on the margin of respectability.

DÉNOUEMENT: The resolution of the plot following the climax.

FAIT ACCOMPLI: A completed and irreversible act.

FEMME FATALE: An alluring woman who leads men into danger.

FEUILLETON: The part of a European newspaper devoted to light fiction and similar articles of general entertainment.

FIN DE SIÈCLE: The end of the nineteenth century.

FLÂNEUR: An idler, loafer.

GENRE: The category of literary work.

HAUT MONDE: High society.

HORS DE COMBAT: "Out of battle," wounded.

MOT JUSTE: Flaubert's term for a precisely appropriate phrase.

NOIR: "Black," usually applied to "dark" suspense novels.

ŒUVRE: An author's body of work.

NOM DE PLUME: A pen name.

NOUVEAU ROMAN: "New novel," an artistic movement led by Alain Robbe-Grillet calling for a new vision of the novel.

RAISONNÉ: Systematically arranged.

ROMAN À CLEF: A novel in which actual persons are disguised as fictional characters.

ROMAN FLEUVE: A long novel chronicling a family or other social group.

ROMAN POLICIER: A police procedural detective novel.

VERS LIBRE: Free verse.

VIGNETTE: A precise intimate literary sketch.

WAGON-LIT: A sleeping compartment in a train.

□ A FEW FRENCH NOMS DE PLUME

Alain-Fournier (Henri Alban Fournier)
Louis Aragon (Louis Andrieux)
Louis-Ferdinand Céline (Louis-Ferdinand Destouches)
Paul Éluard (Eugène Grindel)
Anatole France (Jacques Anatole Thibault)
André Maurois (Emile Herzog)
Pauline Réage (Dominique Aury)
Jules Romains (Louis Farigoule)
Françoise Sagan (Françoise Quoirez)
Saint-John Perse (Alares Léger)
George Sand (Amantine Aurore Dupin)
Georges Simenon (Georges Sim)

Stendhal (Marie-Henry Beyle)
Vercors (Jean Bruller)
Voltaire (François-Marie Arouet)
Marguerite Yourcenar (Marguerite de Crayencour)

□ FIRST WOMAN ELECTED TO THE ACADÉMIE FRANÇAISE

Marguerite Yourcenar

□ THE THREE MUSKETEERS

Athos · Porthos · Aramis

□ GERMAN NOBEL PRIZE WINNERS (LITERATURE)

Heinrich Böll · Rudolf Eucken · Gunter Grass · Gerhart Hauptmann · Herman Hesse · Thomas Mann · Theodor Mommsen · Paul von Heyse

---

□ GERMAN AUTHORS PRONUNCIATION GUIDE

Bertolt Brecht: BER-tawlt BREKT
Peter Handke: PAY-ter HAHNT-keh
Herman Hesse: HARE-mahn HESS-eh
Thomas Mann: TOE-mass MAHN
Karl May: MY
Friedrich Nietzsche: NEE-chuh
Erich Maria Remarque: ruh-MAHRK
Rainer Maria Rilke: RYE-nahr Ma-REE-ah RIHL-kuh
Joseph Roth: Yo-zef ROTE
Johann Wolfgang von Goethe: GER-tuh

□ BEST-SELLING GERMAN AUTHOR OF ALL TIME

Karl May (1842–1912)

☐ SOME GERMAN EVERY READER SHOULD KNOW

Angst: A feeling of anxiety.

Bildungsroman: A "novel of formation"; a novel of someone's growth from childhood to maturity.

Doppelgänger: A ghostly double of a living person, especially one that haunts its own fleshly counterpart.

echt: Genuine, authentic.

ersatz: Artificial, substitute.

Festschrift: A collection of essays published in honor of a distinguished writer.

kitsch: Pretentious bad taste, especially in the arts.

Götterdämmerung: Violent destruction.

Sturm und Drang: German romantic literary movement of the eighteenth century, the works of which typically depicted an impulsive man struggling against conventional society.

Ur-: Prefix indicating original or primitive.

Wanderjahr: "Wander-year": a period in a character's life when he or she leaves her normal routine, and engages in travel and a quest for knowledge.

Wanderlust: A nomadic urge.

Weltanschauung: A comprehensive world view, especially from a specified standpoint.

Weltschmerz: Sadness over the evils of the world.

Zeitgeist: The spirit of the time; the taste and outlook characteristic of a period or generation.

☐ WORLD'S MOST TRANSLATED AUTHOR

V. I. Lenin (3,842 translations)

☐ THE GREAT RUSSIAN NOVELS

According to the Encyclopedia of Culture and Life in Russia *these are the ten greatest Russian novels:*

Eugene Onegin by Aleksander Pushkin
Dead Souls by Nikolai Gogol
Oblomov by Ivan Aleksandrovich Goncharov
Fathers and Sons by Ivan Turgenev
War and Peace by Leo Tolstoy
Anna Karenina by Leo Tolstoy
Crime and Punishment by Fyodor Dostoevesky
The Brothers Karamazov by Fyodor Dostoevesky
Doctor Zhivago by Boris Pasternak
The Master and Margarita by Mikhail Bulgakov

☐ GLOSSARY FOR NINETEENTH-CENTURY RUSSIAN NOVELS

BOYAR: A member of an aristocratic class abolished by Peter I.

COSSACK: A member of a people of southern Russia, noted as fierce cavalrymen.

DACHA: A country villa.

DROSHKY: A four-wheeled, open, horse-drawn carriage.

KOPECK: A coin equal to 1/100 of a ruble.

KVASS: A fermented beverage similar to beer.

INTELLIGENTSIA: The intellectual class.

METROPOLITAN: A primate of an ecclesiastical province of the Orthodox Church.

NOBLE TITLES: Count/countess; duke/duchess; baron/baroness.

MIR: A peasant commune.

PATRONYMIC: Middle name comprised of father's first name and "ovich" for son and "ovna" for daughter.

ROYAL TITLES: Tsar/tsarina (emperor/empress); grand duke/duchess (child or grandchild of a tsar); prince/princess (great grandchild of a tsar).

SAMOVAR: A metal urn with spigot used to boil water for tea.

STEPPE: A treeless grassy plain.

TAIGA: The evergreen forest of Siberia.

TROIKA: A sled drawn by three horses.

TUNDRA: A treeless plain in the Arctic Circle.

VERST: A measure of linear distance, about three-fourths of a mile.

□ RUSSIAN NICKNAMES

Keeping track of characters in Russian novels is hard enough with the patronymics. In addition most Russian first names have diminutives that are used by family and friends. Here are a few:

MEN	WOMEN
Aleksei: Alyosha	Aleksandra: Sasha
Aleksander: Sasha	Anastasia: Nastya
Andrei: Andryusha	Anna: Anya
Boris: Borya	Antonina: Tonya
Dmitri: Dima	Galina: Galya
Fyodor: Fedya	Laresi: Lara
Ivan: Vanya	Mariya: Masha
Mikhail: Misha	Tatiyana: Tanya
Nikolai: Kolya	Yelena: Lena
Sergei: Seryozha	Yevdoheya: Danya
Svyatslav: Slava	

□ FIRST CZECH TO WIN A NOBEL PRIZE

The first – and to date the only – Czech writer awarded the Nobel Prize for Literature is the poet Jaroslav Siefert (1901–1986) who won it in 1984.

☐ THE BEST CZECH LITERATURE

In 1999 the Czech journal Tyden *commissioned a panel of twenty-five literary critics to select the best works of Czech fiction of the twentieth century. These were the top five:*

1. *The Good Soldier Svejk* by Jaroslav Hasek
2. *Too Loud a Solitude* by Bohumil Hrabal
3. *Marketa Lazarova* by Vladislav Vancura
4. *The Cowards* by Josef Skvorecky
5. *The Joke* by Milan Kundera

☐ SPANISH NOBEL PRIZE WINNERS (LITERATURE)

Vicente Alexandre · Jacinto Benavente · Camilo José Cela · José Echegaray y Eizaguirre · Juan Ramón Jiménez

---

☐ SOME PHRASES FROM DON QUIXOTE

A wild goose chase
A finger in every pie
Mind your own business
Thank you for nothing
The pot calling the kettle black
Sky's the limit
Familiarity breeds contempt
Paid in his own coin
Turning over a new leaf
Forgive and forget
Make hay while the sun shines
I have other fish to fry
Honesty is the best policy
All that glistens is not gold
A stone's throw
Give the devil his due

□ PORTUGAL'S NOBEL PRIZE WINNER

In its history of more than one hundred years, the Nobel Prize for literature has been awarded to only one Portuguese author: José Saramago, in 1998.

□ SOME CANADIAN WRITERS

Margaret Atwood · Nick Bantock · Douglas Coupland · Robertson Davies · Charles de Lint · Mazo de la Roche · Joy Fielding · Mavis Gallant · William Gibson · Sparkle Hayter · Barbara Hodgood · Wayne Johnston · W. P. Kinsella · Margaret Laurence · Stephen Leacock · Brett Lott · Malcolm Lowry · Ann-Marie Macdonald · Alistair MacLeod · Stephen Marché · Yann Martel · Rohinton Mistry · L. M. Montgomery · Alice Munro · Michael Ondaatje · Robert Service · Ernest Thompson Seton · Carol Shields · Kate Sterns · Jane Urquhart · Guy Vanderhaeghe · M. G. Vassanji

---

□ MULTIPLE GOVERNOR-GENERAL'S LITERARY AWARD WINNERS (FICTION)

The Governor-General's Award is Canada's preeminent national literary awards and carries a cash prize of $15,000. English-language writers who have won the award more than once since its inception in 1936 are:

Gwethalyn Graham · Margaret Laurence · Hugh MacLennon · Brian Moore · Alice Munro · Michael Ondaatje · Gabrielle Roy · Guy Vanderhaeghe · David Walker

---

□ SOME U.S. WRITERS BORN (OR RAISED) IN CANADA

Charlotte Vale Allen · Saul Bellow · Bliss Carman · Franklin W. Dixon · John Kenneth Galbraith · Malcolm Gladwell · Adam Gopnik · Phyllis McGinley · Robert MacNeil · Charlotte MacLeod · Margaret Millar · Steven Pinsker · Mark Strand · A. E. Van Vogt

□ SOME STEPHEN LEACOCK QUOTES

Advertising may be described as the science of arresting the human intelligence long enough to get money from it.

I detest life-insurance agents; they always argue that I shall some day die, which is not so.

Lord Ronald said nothing; he flung himself from the room, flung himself upon his horse and rode madly off in all directions.

In ancient times they had no statistics so they had to fall back on lies.

It may be that those who do most, dream most.

Personally, I would rather have written *Alice in Wonderland* than the whole *Encyclopædia Brittanica.*

Life, we learn too late, is in the living, the tissue of every day and hour.

Many a man in love with a dimple makes the mistake of marrying the whole girl.

I am a great believer in luck, and find the harder I work the more I have of it.

Men are able to trust one another, knowing the exact degree of dishonesty they are entitled to expect.

The minute a man is convinced he is interesting, he isn't.

A half truth, like half a brick, is always more forcible as an argument than a whole one. It carries better.

Hockey captures the essence of Canadian experience in the New World. In a land so inescapably and inhospitably cold, hockey is the chance of life, and an affirmation that despite the deathly chill of winter, we are alive.

Writing is no trouble: you just jot down ideas as they occur to you. The jotting is simplicity itself – it is the occurring which is difficult.

□ BEST CONTEMPORARY CANADIAN FICTION

Established in 1994, the Giller Prize awards $25,000 annually to the author of the best Canadian novel or short story collection published in English.

2004 Alice Munro, *Runaway*
2003 M. G. Vassanji, *The In-Between World of Vikram Lall*
2002 Austin Clarke, *Polished Hoe*
2001 Richard B. Wright, *Clara Callan*
2000 David Adams Richard, *Mercy Among the Children*
1999 Bonnie Burnard, *A Good House*
1998 Alice Munro, *The Love of a Good Woman*
1997 Mordecai Richler, *Barney's Vision*
1996 Margaret Atwood, *Alias Grace*
1995 Rohinton Mistry, *A Fine Balance*
1994 M. G. Vassanji, *The Book of Secrets*

□ BEST TWENTIETH-CENTURY BRAZILIAN NOVELS

A panel of experts selected by Manchete, *Rio de Janeiro's weekly newspaper, chose their fifty favorite novels of the last century produced by Brazilian writers. Here are the top ten:*

1. *The Devil to Pay in the Backlands* (1956) by João Guimarães Rosa
2. *Macunaíma* (1928) by Mário de Andrade
3. *Policarpo Quaresma's Sad End* (1915) by Lima Barreto
4. *Saint Bernard* (1934) by Graciliano Ramos
5. *The Time and the Wind* (1941) by Erico Verissimo
6. *Maria Moura's Notebook* (1992) by Rachel de Queiroz
7. *Sugar Mill Boy* (1932) by José Lins do Rego
8. *Dead Fire* (1943) by José Lins do Rego
9. *João Miramar's Sentimental Memories* (1924) by Oswald de Andrade
10. *Barren Lives* (1938) by Graciliano Ramos

☐ SOME GREAT LATIN AMERICAN WRITERS

The Premio Miguel de Cervantes (the Cervantes Prize) of 90,000 euros, sometimes referred to as the Spanish Nobel Prize, honors the entire career of an outstanding Spanish-language writer. Past recipients include these writers from Latin America:

Jorge Luis Borges (Argentina) · Guillermo Cabrera Infante (Cuba) · Alejo Carpentier (Cuba) · Adolfo Bioy Casares (Argentina) · Carlos Fuentes (Mexico) · Octavio Paz (Mexico) · Mario Vargas Llosa (Peru)

☐ FIVE GREAT MEXICAN BOOKS

Earl Shorris, author of Latinos: A Biography of the People, *selected five great works of Mexican literature for Salon.com:*

The Labyrinth of Solitude by Octavio Paz
Aztec Thought and Culture by Miguel Len-Portilla
Memories of Pancho Villa by Martín Luis Guzmán
Pedro Paramo by Juan Rulfo
The Death of Artemio Cruz by Carlos Fuentes

☐ SPANISH-AMERICAN NOBEL PRIZE WINNERS (LITERATURE)

Miguel Angel Asturias (Guatemala) · Gabriel García Márquez (Colombia) · Gabriela Mistral (Chile) · Pablo Neruda (Chile)

☐ SOME CARIBBEAN-BORN AUTHORS

Reinaldo Arenas (Cuba) · John James Audubon (Dominican Republic) · Alejo Carpentier (Cuba) · Austin Clarke (Barbados) · Michelle Cliff (Barbados) · Judith Ortiz Cofer (Puerto Rico) · Victor Hernández Cruz (Puerto Rico) · Fred D'Aguilar (Guyana) · Edwidge Danticat (Haiti) · Junot Díaz (Dominican Republic) · Rosario Ferre (Puerto Rico) · Cristina García (Cuba) · Carolina Garcia-Aguilera (Cuba) · Rosa Guy (Trinidad) · Jamaica Kincaid (Antigua) · José Lezama Lima (Cuba) · Earl Lovelace (Trinidad) · Claude McKay (Jamaica) · Pauline Melville (Guyana) · V. S.

JORGE LUIS BORGES

Naipaul (Trinidad) · Caryl Phillips (St. Kitts) · Nelly Rosario (Dominican Republic) · Miguel Piñero (Puerto Rico) · Jean Rhys (Dominica) · Louis Simpson (Jamaica) · Saint-John Perse (Guadeloupe) · Derek Walcott (Saint Lucia) · Edgar Vega Yunqué (Puerto Rico)

☐ CLASSIC NOVELS OF BLACK AFRICA

This list was put together by the Queens Borough (New York City) Public Library.

Chinua Achebe (Nigeria) *Things Fall Apart*
Peter Abrahams (South Africa) *Mine Boy*
Ama Ata Aidoo (Ghana) *Our Sister Killjoy*
Elechi Amadi (Nigeria) *The Concubine*
Ayi Kwei Armah (Ghana) *The Beautiful Ones Are Not Yet Born*
Kofi Awoonor (Ghana) *This Earth, My Brother...*
Mariama Bâ (Senegal) *Scarlet Song*
Mongo Beti (Cameroon) *Mission to Kala*
Birago Diop (Senegal) *Tales of Amadou Koumba*
T. Obinkaram Echewa (Nigeria) *I Saw the Sky Catch Fire*
Cyprian Ekwensi (Nigeria) *Jagua Nana*
Buchi Emecheta (Nigeria) *The Bride Price*
Aminata Sow Fall (Senegal) *The Beggars' Strike*
Bessie Head (South Africa) *Maru*
Cheikh Hamidou Kane (Senegal) *Ambiguous Adventure*
Wilson Katiyo (Zimbabwe) *A Son of the Soil*
Alex LaGuma (South Africa) *In the Fog of the Season's End*
Thomas Mofolo (South Africa) *Chaka*
Ngugi wa Thiong'o (Kenya) *A Grain of Wheat*
D. T. Niane (Mali) *Sundiata: An Epic of Old Mali*
Flora Nwapa (Nigeria) *Efuru*
Ben Okri (Nigeria) *Flowers and Shadows*
Sembene Ousmane (Senegal) *God's Bits of Wood*
Ferdinand Oyono (Cameroon) *Houseboy*
Wole Soyinka (Nigeria) *The Interpreters*
Amos Tutuola (Nigeria) *The Palm Wine Drinkard*

□ INDIAN AUTHOR PRONUNCIATION GUIDE

Sunetra Gupta: Shu-NET-rah GUP-tah
Ruth Prawer Jhabvala: PRAH-ver JAHB-vah-lah
V. S. Naipaul: nie-PAWL
Salmon Rushdie: RUSH-dee (as in "push")
Rabindranath Tagore: tuh-GOHR
Jhumpa Lahiri: JUME-pah Lah-EE-rie
Amit Chaudhuri: chawd-HOO-ree
Vikram Seth: SATE

□ PACIFIC RIM BOOKS

The $30,000 Kiriyama Prize is awarded annually by the Kiriyama Pacific Rim Institute for books that contribute to "greater understanding and cooperation among the peoples and nations of the Pacific Rim and South Asia."

2004 Nadeem Aslam, *Maps for Lost Lovers*
Soketo Mehta, *Maximum City: Bombay Lost and Found*
2003 Shan Sa, *The Girl Who Played Go*
Inga Clendinnen, *Dancing with Strangers*
2002 Rohinton Mistry, *Family Matters*
Pascal Khoo Thwe, *From the Land of Green Ghost: A Burmese Odyssey*
2001 Patricia Grace, *Dogride Story*
Peter Hessler, *River Town*
2000 Michael Ondaatje, *Anil's Ghost*
David Michael Kwan, *Things That Must Not Be Forgotten: A Childhood in Wartime China*
1999 Chen Ch'ing-wen, *Three-Legged Horse*
Anchee X. Pham, *Catfish and Mandala: A Two-Wheeled Journey through the Landscape and Memory of Vietnam*
1998 Ruth L. Ozeki, *My Year of Meats*
1997 Patricia Smith, *Japan: A Reinterpretation*
1996 Alan Brown, *Audrey Hepburn's Neck*

SOME ASIAN-BORN WRITERS IN THE UNITED STATES

Mei-Mei Berssenbrugge (China) · Peter Carey (Australia) · Leslie Charteris (Singapore) · Marilyn Chin (Hong Kong) · Tinling Choong (Malaysia) · Jill Ker Conway (Australia) · Anita Desai (India) · Chita Divakaruni (India) · Amitav Ghosh (India) · Kahlil Gibran (Lebanon) · Jessica Hagedorn (Philippines) · Shirley Hazzard (Australia) · Ha Jin (China) · Khaled Hosseini (Afghanistan) · C. Y. Lee (China) · Chang-rae Lee (Korea) · Shirley Geok-Lin Lim (Malaysia) · Bette Bao Lord (China) · Ved Mehta (India) · Anchee Min (China) · Kyoko Mori (Japan) · Bharati Mukherjee (India) · Azar Nafisi (Iran) · Gina Nahai (Iran) · Kien Nguyen (Vietnam) · Edward Said (Palestine) · Akhil Sharma (India) · Hilary Than (Malaysia) · Loung Ung (Cambodia) · Mary Yukari Waters (Japan) · Geling Yan (China)

THE FIRST NOVEL

The first full-fledged novel is Lady Murasaki's *The Tale of Genji* (c. 1011), a chronicle of tenth-century Japanese court life.

EDGAR AWARD GRAND MASTERS

The Mystery Writers of America singles out the most accomplished authors in the mystery field for "Grand Master" recognition.

Eric Ambler · Lawrence Block · W. R. Burnett · James M. Cain · John Dickinson Carr · Agatha Christie · Mary Higgins Clark · George Harmon Coxe · John Creasey · Dorothy Salisbury Davis · Daphne du Maurier · Mignon G. Eberhart · Stanley Ellin · Dick Francis · Erle Stanley Gardner · Michael Gilbert · Graham Greene · Tony Hillerman · Edward D. Hoch · Dorothy B. Hughes · P. D. James · Baynard Kendrick · John Le Carré · Elmore Leonard · Ira Levin · Ross Macdonald · Ed McBain · Helen

McCloy · Ngaio Marsh · Barbara Mertz · Margaret Muller · Marcia Muller · Robert B. Parker · Ellery Queen · Ruth Rendell · Georges Simenon · Mickey Spillane · Aaron Marc Stein · Vincent Starrett · Rex Stout · Julian Symons · Joseph Wambaugh · Hilary Waugh · Donald Westlake · Phyllis A. Whitney

---

☐ IMBA BEST MYSTERIES

The Dilys Award has been given each year since 1993 by the Independent Mystery Booksellers Association to the mystery title which the member booksellers most enjoyed selling. Recipients include:

2004 Jasper Fforde, *Lost in a Good Book*
2003 Julia Spencer-Fleming, *In the Bleak Midwinter*
2002 Dennis Lehane, *Mystic River*
2001 Val McDermid, *A Place of Execution*
2000 Robert Crais, *L.A. Requiem*
1998 Janet Evanovich, *Three to Get Deadly*
1997 Michael Connelly, *The Poet*
1996 Michael Connelly, *The Last Coyote*
1995 Janet Evanovich, *One for the Money*
1994 Peter Høeg, *Smilla's Sense of Snow*
1993 John Dunning, *Booked to Die*
1992 Carl Hiaasen, *Native Tongue*

☐ WHOPUNITS

No other genre so abounds in whimsical titles as crime fiction. Both cunning and punning are helpful in marketing mysteries. Here are some of the least execrable puns of actual mysteries:

Morgue the Merrier · Half-Past Mortem · Three Short Biers · Dewey Decimated · Remains to Be Seen · Widow's Pique · A Time to Prey · Board Stiff · Corpse de Ballet · Bones of Contention · Abracadaver · Stab in the Dark · Some Like 'Em Shot · The Dead of Winter · Sudden Death

☐ MYSTERY SUBGENRES

According to the folks at www.mysteryguide.com, these are the sub-genres of the mystery novel:

caper · classic whodunit · cozy · espionage · forensic · hard-boiled · historical · legal military · police procedural · political · private eye · serial killer · sci-fi mystery · special subject · suspense · thriller

---

☐ MULTIPLE ANTHONY AWARD WINNERS

Named after the distinguished mystery critic Anthony Boucher (1911-1968), Anthony Awards are given annually at the Boucheron World Mystery Convention. Since it was established in 1986 only two authors have won multiple awards for best novel:

Michael Connelly · Sue Grafton

☐ THE GRAFTON ABECEDARY

Sue Grafton launched her Kinsey Milhone detective novel series in 1982 with "A" is for Alibi *and has been marching through the alphabet since.*

Alibi · Burglar · Corpse · Deadbeat · Evidence · Fugitive · Gumshoe · Homicide · Innocent · Judgment · Killer · Lawless · Malice · Noose · Outlaw · Peril · Quarry · Ricochet · Silence

---

☐ SOME CRIME AUTHORS' HOME PAGES

David Baldacci: *david-baldacci.com*
Lawrence Block: *lawrenceblock.com*
Rita Mae Brown: *ritamaebrown.org*
Robert Crais: *robertcrais.com*
Stephen J. Cannell: *cannell.com*
Michael Connelly: *michaelconnelly.com*
Patricia Cornwell: *patriciacornwell.com*
Jeffery Deaver: *jefferydeaver.com*

Nelson Demille: *nelsondemille.net*
James Ellroy: *ellroy.com*
Janet Evanovich: *evanovich.com*
Linda Fairstein: *lindafairstein.com*
Elizabeth George: *elizabethgeorgeonline.com*
Sue Grafton: *suegrafton.com*
Martha Grimes: *marthagrimes.com*
John Grisham: *randomhouse.com/features/grisham*
Greg Iles: *gregiles.com*
Stuart Kaminsky: *stuartkaminsky.com*
Laurie R. King: *laurierking.com*
John Le Carré: *johnlecarre.com*
Dennis Lehane: *dennislehanebooks.com*
Laura Lippman: *lauralippman.com*
Sara Paretsky: *saraparetsky.com*
T. Jefferson Parker: *tjeffersonparker.com*
Ridley Pearson: *ridleypearson.com*
Peter Robinson: *inspectorbanks.com*
John Sandford: *johnsandford.org*
Lisa Scottoline: *scottoline.com*
Julie Smith: *juliesmith.com*
Scott Turow: *scottturow.com*
Andrew Vachss: *vachss.com*
Laura Van Wormer: *lauravanwormer.com*
Stuart Woods: *stuartwoods.com*

□ MOST PROLIFIC MYSTERY WRITER

John Creasey (1908-73) published 562 full-length books under twenty-nine pen names.

□ SOME PEN NAMES USED BY DEAN KOONTZ

David Axton · Brian Coffey · Deanna Dwyer · K. R. Dwyer · John Hill · Leigh Nichols · Anthony North · Richard Paige · Owen West · Aaron Wolfe

☐ SOME SUSPENSE WRITERS' REAL NAMES

Catherine Aird (Kinn McIntosh)
Bruce Alexander (Bruce Cook)
Russell Andrews (Peter Gethers)
Evelyn Anthony (Evelyn Ward Thomas)
M. C. Beaton (Marion Chesney)
Anthony Berkeley (A. B. Cox)
Nicholas Blake (Cecil Day-Lewis)
Michael Collins (Dennis Lynds)
Edmund Crispin (Bruce Montgomery)
Amanda Cross (Carolyn Heilbrun)
E. V. Cunningham (Howard Fast)
Lillian de la Torre (Lillian Bueno McCue)
E. X. Ferrars (Moura Brown)
Nicolas Freeling (F. R. Nicholas)
Jonathan Gash (John Grant)
Anthony Gilbert (Lucy Malleson)
Adam Hall (Ellston Trevor)
Brett Halliday (Davis Dresser)
Gar Anthony Haywood (Ray Shannon)
Jack Higgins (Harry Patterson)
Michael Innes (J. I. M. Stewart)
Frances Iles (Anthony Cox)
Emma Lathem (Mary J. Latsis & Martha Hennisart)
Ross Macdonald (Kenneth Millar)
Judith Michael (Judith Barbard & Michael Fain)
Perri O'Shaughnessy (Pamela & Mary O'Shaughnessy)
Hugh Pentecost (Judson Phillips)
Ellis Peters (Edith Pargeter)
Ellery Queen (Frederic Dannay & Manfred B. Lee)
Craig Rice (Georgina Ann Randolph)
S. J. Rozan (Shira Rosan)
John Sandford (John Camp)
Dell Shannon (Elizabeth Linnington)
Richard Stark (Donald Westlake)
Josphine Tey (Elizabeth MacKintosh)

Trevanian (Rodney Whitaker)
S. S. Van Dine (Willard H. Wright)
Barbara Vine (Ruth Rendell)
Sara Woods (Sarah Bowen-Judd)
Margaret Yorke (Margaret Nicholson)

□ TOP HARD-BOILED CHARACTERS OF THE TWENTIETH CENTURY

In 2002 the members of Rara-Avis, a Web discussion group for all things hard-boiled, voted on the top one hundred hard-boiled characters. Here are the top ten:

1. Philip Marlowe (Raymond Chandler)
2. Sam Spade (Dashiell Hammett)
3. The Continental Op (Dashiell Hammett)
4. Lew Archer (Ross Macdonald)
5. Matt Scudder (Lawrence Block)
6. Parker (Richard Stark)
7. Travis McGee (Ross MacDonald)
8. Easy Rawlins (Walter Mosley)
9. Harry Bosch (Michael Connelly)
10. Hoke Moseley (Charles Willeford)

□ FATHER OF THE MYSTERY

Edgar Allan Poe (1809–1849). Poe's story "The Murders in the Rue Morgue" was published in 1841. The crime was solved by Chevalier C. Auguste Dupin who would appear in five subsequent stories. These stories became the foundation of the modern mystery novel.

□ FIRST MYSTERY SERIES WITH A FEMALE PROFESSIONAL SLEUTH

Zelda Popkin (1898–1983) may have been the first mystery writer to feature a young woman as a private detective, namely, Mary Carner, starting with *Death Wears a White Gardenia* (1938).

RAYMOND CHANDLER

☐ SOME RAYMOND CHANDLER QUIPS

Chandler's Philip Marlowe detective novels set the standard for later noirish writers of the genre. His similes and one-liners are original and funny.

The kid's face had as much expression as a cut of round steak and was about the same color.

From thirty feet away she looked like a lot of class. From ten feet away she looked like something made up to be seen from thirty feet away.

The General spoke again, slowly, using his strength as carefully as an out-of–work show-girl uses her last pair of stockings.

Even on Central Avenue, not the quietest dressed street in the world, he looked about as inconspicuous as a tarantula on a slice of angel food.

It was a blonde. A blonde to make a bishop kick a hole in a stained glass window.

On the dance floor half a dozen couples were throwing themselves around with the reckless abandon of a night watchman with arthritis.

To say she had a face that would have stopped a clock would have been an insult to her. It would have stopped a runaway horse.

I called him from a phone booth. The voice that answered was fat. It wheezed softly, like the voice of a man who had just won a pie-eating contest.

The minutes went by on tiptoe, with their fingers to their lips.

Her smile was as faint as a fat lady at a fireman's ball.

I'm an occasional drinker, the kind of guy who goes out for a beer and wakes up in Singapore with a full beard.

I belonged in Idle Valley like a pearl onion on a banana split.

She smelled the way the Taj Mahal looks by moonlight.

☐ TRAVIS MCGEE COLORS

Here are the colorful titles of John D. MacDonald's twenty-one-book detective series featuring Travis McGee:

The Deep Blue Good-By
Nightmare in Pink
A Purple Place for Dying
The Quick Red Fox
A Deadly Shade of Gold
Bright Orange for the Shroud
Darker than Amber
One Fearful Yellow Eye
Pale Gray for Guilt
Dress Her in Indigo
The Girl in the Plain Brown Wrapper
The Long Lavender Look
A Tan and Sandy Silence
The Scarlet Ruse
The Turquoise Lament
The Dreadful Lemon Sky
The Empty Copper Sea
The Green Ripper
Free Fall in Crimson
Cinnamon Skin
The Lonely Silver Rain

☐ BEST AUDIO MYSTERIES

Each year the Audio Publishers Association presents "Audies" for the best audio books of the year in a variety of categories, including mysteries:

2005 *Selected Unabridged Stories* by Jeffery Deaver, various readers
2004 *Lost Light* by Michael Connelly, read by Len Cariou
2003 *Jolie Blon's Bounce* by James Lee Burke, read by Will Patton
2002 *Tell No One* by Harlan Coben, read by Steven Weber
2001 *The Naked Detective* by Laurence Shames, read by Ron McLarty
2000 *The Breaker* by Minette Walters, read by Robert Powell
1999 *The Third Man* by Graham Greene, read by Martin Jarvis
1998 *Vintage Crime Stories* by Ruth Rendell, et al., read by Patrick Malahide
1997 *The Mysterious Affair at Styles* by Agatha Christie, read by David Suchet

☐ LONGEST-RUNNING AMERICAN DETECTIVE SERIES (BY NUMBER OF NOVELS)

Series	Author	Number	Time Span
Mike Shayne	Brett Halliday	77	1939–76
Ed Noon	Michael Avallone	35?	1953–88
Shell Scott	Richard S. Prather	35	1950–87
Spenser	Robert P. Parker	32	1973–
Rick Holman	Carter Brown	31	1961–76
Danny Boyd	Carter Brown	30?	1956–84
Bertha Cool & Donald Lam	A. A. Fair	29	1939–70
Johnny Liddell	Frank Kane	29	1947–67
Peter Chambers	Henry Kane	29	1947–72
Nameless	Bill Pronzini	28	1971–

☐ LONGEST-RUNNING AMERICAN DETECTIVE SERIES (BY TIME SPAN)

The Dan Fortune series by Michael Collins, which ran from 1967 to 2004.

☐ FIRST DETECTIVE TO APPEAR IN AN ENGLISH NOVEL

Inspector Bucket of the London police force in Charles Dickens's *Bleak House*, 1852–1853.

☐ MOVIES MADE FROM ELMORE LEONARD NOVELS

Hombre (1961)
The Big Bounce (1969)
The Moonshine War (1969)
Valdez Is Coming (1970)
Stick (1983)
52 Pick-Up (1974)
Cat Chaser (1982)
Touch (1987)
Get Shorty (1991)
Jackie Brown (1997)
Out of Sight (1996)
Be Cool (1999)

☐ GLOSSARY FOR READERS OF BRITISH CRIME NOVELS

AGGRO: Aggravation, violence.

ANORAK: A geek, a nerd, a "trainspotter."

BOB'S YOUR UNCLE: And so it is done.

BUGGER OFF: To tell someone to go away.

(TO DO A) BUNK: To escape.

CHIPPY: A fish and chip shop.

TRAINERS: Running shoes.

CID: Criminal investigation department.

CUSHY: Easy.

DC: Detective constable.

DCI: Detective chief inspector.

DI: Detective inspector.

DS: Detective sergeant.

DODGY: Dubious (of a thing or person).

(THE) FILTH: Police.

GOBSHITE: Someone who talks rubbish.

GOBSMACKED: Surprised.

GRASS UP: Inform on.

GUV'NOR OR GUV: Boss or chief.

HANDLER: An officer in charge of informant.

KIP: Sleep.

KNACKERED: Exhausted.

KNOCKING SHOP: A brothel.

MANOR: Territory, "turf."

(THE) NICK: A police station or prison.

NONCE: A sex offender.

NUTTER: Someone crazy or violent.

OFFIE: Off-license, liquor store.

PISS-UP: A drinking bout.

PISSED: Drunk.

POSH: Fashionable, smart.

PONCE: A very flashy person.

PUNTER: A member of the paying public, a customer.

RUMBLED: Found out.

(DO A) RUNNER: Leave the scene of a crime quickly.

SARKY: Sarcastic.

SLAG: Loose woman, a tart.

SUITS: CID officers.

WANKER: An idiot.

☐ THE CARTIER DIAMOND DAGGER LIFETIME ACHIEVEMENT AWARD

Annually since 1986, the British Crime Writers Association has selected a writer whose career is marked by sustained excellence and has made a significant contribution to crime fiction published in the English language. Honorees are:

Eric Ambler · Robert Barnard · Lawrence Block · Leslie Charteris · Lionel Davidson · Colin Dexter · Dick Francis · Michael Gilbert · Reginald Hill · P. D. James · H. F. R. Keating · John Le Carré · Peter Lovesey · Ed McBain · Sara Paretsky · Ellis Peters · Ian Rankin · Ruth Rendell · Julian Symons · Margaret Yorke

---

☐ SCI-FI SUBGENRES

alien beings · magic · alternate/parallel worlds · new wave · alternate history · parody · apocalypse · quest · Arthurian legend · robots/androids/cyborgs · colonization/terrafarming · saga/myth/legend · cyberpunk · shared worlds · dystopia/utopia · space travel · galactic empires/space operas · steam punk · hard science · sword & sorcery · lost worlds · time travel

□ THE WISDOM OF TERRY PRATCHETT

The British sci-fi/fantasy author is one of the biggest-selling writers in the world. He is also one of the funniest.

An ancient proverb summed it up: when a wizard is tired of looking for broken glass in his dinner, it ran, he is tired of life.

Build a man a fire, and he'll be warm for a day. Set a man on fire, and he'll be warm the rest of his life.

Fantasy is an exercise bicycle for the mind. It might not take you anywhere, but it tones up the muscles that can.

Only in our dreams are we free. The rest of the time we need wages.

The universe, they said, depended for its operation on the balance of four forces which they identified as charm, persuasion, uncertainty and bloody-mindedness.

They say a little knowledge is a dangerous thing, but it's not one-half so bad as a lot of ignorance.

He was the sort of person who stood on mountaintops during thunderstorms in wet copper armor shouting, "All the Gods are bastards."

People who are rather more than six feet tall and nearly as broad across the shoulders often have an unhelpful item that weighs less than its operating manual.

One of the universal rules of happiness is: always be wary of any eventful journeys. People jump out at them from behind rocks then say things like, "Oh. Sorry. I thought you were someone else."

Of course, I could be wrong.

That seems to point up a significant difference between Europeans and Americans. A European says: "I can't understand this, what's wrong with me?" An American says: "I can't understand this, what's wrong with him?"

You can't trample infidels when you're a tortoise. I mean, all you could do is give them a meaningful look.

This isn't life in the fast lane. This is life in oncoming traffic.

□ MULTIPLE "HUGO" WINNERS

The Hugo Award, named in honor of Hugo Gernsback, "The Father of Magazine Science Fiction," is given annually by the World Science Fiction Society. Since its inception in 1953, the following writers have won more than once for best novel:

Isaac Asimov · David Brin · Lois McMaster Bujold · Orson Scott Card · C. J. Cherryh · Arthur C. Clarke · Joe Haldeman · Robert Heinlein · Ursula K. Le Guin · Fritz Leiber · Kim Stanley Robinson · Vernon Vinge · Connie Willis · Roger Zelazny

---

□ SOME SCI-FI/FANTASY WRITERS' REAL NAMES

Hal Clement (Harry Stubbs)
Larry Niven (Laurence Van Cott)
André Norton (Alice Mary Norton)
Lewis Padgett (Henry Kuttner)
Robert Jordan (James O. Rigney, Jr.)
Cordwainer Smith (Paul Lineburger)
Theodore Sturgeon (Edward Waldo)
James Tiptree, Jr. (Alice Sheldon)
John Wyndham (John Harris)

□ SCI-FI GRAND MASTERS

Since 1974 the Science Fiction and Fantasy Writers of America has bestowed its Grand Master award to a living author for a lifetime's achievement. The winners:

2004 Anne McCaffrey
2003 Robert Silverberg
2002 Ursula K. Le Guin

2000 Philip José Farmer
1999 Brian W. Aldiss
1998 Hal Clement
1997 Poul Anderson
1996 Jack Vance
1994 Damon Knight
1992 Frederick Pohl
1990 Lester Del Rey
1988 Ray Bradbury
1987 Alfred Bester
1986 Isaac Asimov
1985 Arthur C. Clarke
1983 Andre Norton
1981 Fritz Leiber
1978 L. Sprague de Camp
1976 Clifford D. Simak
1975 Jack Williamson
1974 Robert A. Heinlein

□ MULTIPLE NEBULA AWARD WINNERS

The annual Nebula Award for best novel is chosen by the Science Fiction and Fantasy Writers of America. Authors who have received the award more than once are:

Greg Bear · Orson Scott Card · Arthur C. Clarke · Samuel Delaney · Ursula K. Le Guin · Vonda N. McIntyre · Frederick Pohl

---

□ SOME FILMS MADE FROM PHILIP K. DICK NOVELS AND SHORT STORIES

Next (2006) based on "The Golden Man"
A Scanner Darkly (2005) based on *A Scanner Darkly*
Paycheck (2003) based on "Paycheck"
Minority Report (2002) based on "The Minority Report"
Impostor (2001) based on "Impostor"
Confessions d'un Bario (1992) based on *Confessions of a Crap Artist*

Total Recall (1990) based on "We Can Remember It for You Wholesale"
Screamers (1996) based on "Second Variety"
Blade Runner (1992) based on *Do Androids Dream of Electric Sheep?*

□ BEST HORROR NOVELS

The Bram Stoker Awards, named in honor of the author of Dracula, *are presented annually by the Horror Writers Association for superior achievement in horror.*

2004 Peter Straub, *In the Night Room*
2003 Peter Straub, *lost boy lost girl*
2002 Tom Piccirilli, *The Night Class*
2001 Neil Gaiman, *American Gods*
2000 Richard Laymon, *The Traveling Vampire Show*
1999 Peter Straub, *Mr. X*
1998 Stephen King, *Bag of Bones*
1997 Janet Berliner & George Guthridge, *Children of the Dusk*
1996 Stephen King, *The Green Mile*
1995 Joyce Carol Oates, *Zombie*
1994 Nancy Holder, *Dead in the Water*
1993 Peter Straub, *The Throat*
1992 Thomas F. Monteleone, *Blood of the Lamb*
1991 Robert R. McCammon, *Boy's Life*
1990 Robert McCammon, *Mine*
1989 Dan Simmons, *Carrion Comfort*
1988 Thomas Harris, *The Silence of the Lambs*
1987 Stephen King, *Misery*, & Robert McCammon, *Swan Song*

□ SOME HORROR WRITERS' OFFICIAL WEB SITES

Clive Barker: *clivebarker.com*
Ramsey Campbell: *ramseycampbell.com*
Harlan Ellison: *harlanellison.com*
Neil Gaiman: *neilgaiman.com*

Thomas Harris: *randomhouse.com/features/thomasharris.home*
Stephen King: *stephenking.com*
Robert McCammon: *robertmccammon.com*
Dan Simmons: *dansimmons.com*
Peter Straub: *peterstraub.net*

☐ LIFETIME ACHIEVEMENT

The Bram Stoker Award for Lifetime Achievement is presented periodically by the Horror Writers Association to an individual whose work has substantially influenced the horror genre.

2004 Michael Moorcock
2003 Anne Rice; Martin H. Greenberg
2002 Stephen King; J. N. Williamson
2001 John Farris
2000 Nigel Kneale
1999 Edward Gorey; Charles L. Grant
1998 Ramsey Campbell
1997 William Peter Blatty; Jack Williamson
1996 Ira Levin; Forrest J. Ackerman
1995 Harlan Ellison
1994 Christopher Lee
1993 Joyce Carol Oates
1992 Ray Russell
1991 Gahan Wilson
1990 Hugh B. Cave
1989 Robert Bloch
1988 Ray Bradbury
1987 Fritz Leiber; Frank Belknap Long; Clifford D. Simak

☐ FEATURE FILMS BASED ON STEPHEN KING'S FICTION

Carrie (1976)
The Shining (1980)
The Dead Zone (1983)
Christine (1983)
Cujo (1983)

STEPHEN KING

Children of the Corn (1984)
Firestarter (1984)
Silver Bullet (1985)
Cat's Eye (1985)
Maximum Overdrive (1986)
Stand by Me (1986)
Creepshow 2 (1987)
A Return to Salem's Lot (1987)
The Running Man (1987)
Pet Sematary (1989)
Graveyard Shift (1990)
Misery (1990)
Children of the Corn II: The Final Sacrifice (1992)
The Lawnmower Man (1992)
Pet Semetary II (1992)
Sleepwalkers (1992)
The Dark Half (1993)
Needful Things (1993)
Children of the Corn III: Urban Harvest (1994)
Dolores Claiborne (1994)
The Shawshank Redemption (1994)
The Mangler (1995)
Sometimes They Come Back . . . Again (1996)
Children of the Corn IV: The Gathering (1996)
Thinner (1996)
The Night Flier (1997)
Trucks (1998)
Children of the Corn V: Fields of Terror (1998)
Apt Pupil (1998)
Children of the Corn 666: Isaac's Return (1999)
The Green Mile (1999)
Paranoid (2000)
Children of the Corn 7: Revelation (2001)
The Mangler 2 (2001)
Hearts in Atlantis (2001)
Secret Window (2004)
Stephen King's Riding the Bullet (2004)
The Talisman (2005)

☐ SOME MEMORABLE CLOSING LINES

But no, he would not give in. Turning sharply, he walked towards the city's gold phosphorescence. His fists were shut, his mouth set fast. He would not take that direction, to the darkness, to follow her. He walked towards the faintly humming, glowing town, quickly. – D. H. Lawrence, *Sons and Lovers*

We must cultivate our garden. – Voltaire, *Candide*

It is a far, far better thing that I do than I have ever done; it is a far, far better rest that I go to than I have ever known.
– Charles Dickens, *A Tale of Two Cities*

After all, tomorrow is another day.
– Margaret Mitchell, *Gone With the Wind*

And oh, Aunt Em! I'm so glad to be at home again!
– L. Frank Baum, *The Wonderful Wizard of Oz*

He turned now with a lover's thirst, to images of tranquil skies, fresh meadows, cool brooks; an existence of soft and eternal peace. – Stephen Crane, *The Red Badge of Courage*

And so we beat on, boats against the current, borne back ceaselessly into the past. – F. Scott Fitzgerald, *The Great Gatsby*

That was all long ago in some brief lost spring, in a place that is no more. In that hour that frogs begin and the scent off the mesquite comes strongest.
– Nelson Algren, *A Walk on the Wild Side*

I been there before. – Mark Twain, *Huckleberry Finn*

The offing was barred by a black bank of clouds, and the tranquil waterway leading to the uttermost ends of the earth flowed sombre under an overcast sky – seemed to lead into the heart of an immense darkness. – Joseph Conrad, *Heart of Darkness*

Turning him over one saw that he could not have suffered long; his face had an expression of calm, as though almost glad the end had come. – Erich Maria Remarque,
All Quiet on the Western Front

And it may be that sometimes love occurs without pain or misery. – E. Annie Proulx, *The Shipping News*

Out of this universal feast of death, out of this extremity of fever, kindling the rain-washed evening sky to a fiery glow, may it be that Love one day shall mount?
– Thomas Mann, *The Magic Mountain*

Matter of fact, I think this the youngest us ever felt. Amen.
– Alice Walker, *The Color Purple*

Taking the pigtail in one of his paws, he pressed it warmly to his wet moustache. – John Kennedy Toole, *A Confederacy of Dunces*

At that, as if it had been the signal he waited for, Newland Archer got up slowly and walked back alone to his hotel.
– Edith Wharton, *Age of Innocence*

I lingered round them, under that benign sky; watched the moths fluttering among the heath and hare-bells; listened to the soft wind breathing through the grass; and wondered how anyone could ever imagine unquiet slumbers for the sleepers in that quiet earth. – Emily Brontë, *Wuthering Heights*

April 27 Old father, old artificer, stand me now and ever in good stead. – James Joyce, *A Portrait of the Artist as a Young Man*

She looked up and across the barn, and her lips came together and smiled mysteriously. – John Steinbeck, *The Grapes of Wrath*

When the long winter nights come on and the wolves follow their meat into the lower valleys, he may be seen running at the head of the pack through the pale moonlight or glimmering borealis, leaping gigantic above his fellows or throat a-bellow as he sings a song of the younger world, which is the song of the pack. Jack London, *The Call of the Wild*

"Now vee may perhaps to begin. Yes?
– Philip Roth, *Portnoy's Complaint*

That might be the subject of a new story, but our present story is ended. – Fyodor Dostoevsky, *Crime and Punishment*

□ FAMOUS LAST WORDS

Edgar Allan Poe: Lord help my soul.

Dylan Thomas: I've had eighteen straight whiskies. I think that's a record.

James Joyce: Does nobody understand?

Henry David Thoreau: I leave the world without a regret the fair is over.

Oscar Wilde: Either the wallpaper goes, or I do.

Robert Burns: Don't let the awkward squad fire over my head.

Lord Byron: Now I shall go to sleep.

Thomas Carlyle: So this is Death – well –.

Voltaire: Do let me die in peace.

François Rabelais: Let down the curtain.

J. W. von Goethe: More light!

Blaise Pascal: My God, forsake me not.

ABOUT THE AUTHOR

For twenty-five years, bibliotopian STEVEN GILBAR has been writing about books and reading. His "book books" include *The Book Book, Good Books, The Reader's Quotation Book, Reading in Bed,* and *Published and Perished.* He is also the editor of the short-story anthologies *California Shorts, L. A. Shorts, Santa Barbara Stories* and *Americans in Paris.* Since retiring as an attorney, he has been able to devote more time to his passion and avocation: reading good books. Mr. Gilbar lives in Santa Barbara, California with his wife, the mental health activist Inge Gatz.

ABOUT THE ARTIST

Born in California in 1945, Elliott Banfield attended Columbia College, studied architecture for a time, was drafted into the United States Army for two uneventful years, and finally settled in New York City's Lower East Side, with vague ambitions of becoming an artist.

Mr. Banfield's career as an illustrator began in the early 1970s, when the *American Spectator* first published his drawings. During the 1980s and early '90s, he contributed drawings on a weekly basis to the *New York Times Book Review*, moving on to provide illustrations for the *New York Times*, portraits for the *Wall Street Journal*, and illustrations for two novels by J. P. Donleavy.

Since the late 1990s Mr. Banfield has come to embrace the possibilities offered by the digital age. He has created large color prints on architectural subjects, and has gone on to design and illustrate the *Claremont Review of Books*, a quarterly edited by Charles Kesler. Starting in 2005 he contributed editorial cartoons to the *New York Sun*. The decorations for the present volume were created by means of the Macintosh G5 computer and software from Adobe Systems Incorporated.

A NOTE ON THE TYPE

BIBLIOTOPIA has been set in Kepler, a multiple-master typeface designed by Robert Slimbach for Adobe in 1996. Rooted in the so-called modern types of the late eighteenth century, Kepler was designed to be free of the coldness and formality of its forebears while capitalizing on their refined appearance. Its multiple-master features – variable weight, width, and optical size – make it an unusually adaptable type, well suited to a broad range of typographic purposes and compositional styles.

Design and composition by Carl W. Scarbrough

Venetian	*French*	*Dutch-English*	*Transitional*	*Modern*
N *N*	N *N*	N *N*	N *N*	N *N*
O *O*	O *O*	O *O*	O *O*	O *O*
P *P*	P *P*	P *P*	P *P*	P *P*
Q *Q*	Q *Q*	Q *Q*	Q *Q*	Q *Q*
R *R*	R *R*	R *R*	R *R*	R *R*
S *S*	S *S*	S *S*	S *S*	S *S*
T *T*	T *T*	T *T*	T *T*	T *T*
U *U*	U *U*	U *U*	U *U*	U *U*
V *V*	V *V*	V *V*	V *V*	V *V*
W *W*	W *W*	W *W*	W *W*	W *W*
X *X*	X *X*	X *X*	X *X*	X *X*
Y *Y*	Y *Y*	Y *Y*	Y *Y*	Y *Y*
Z *Z*	Z *Z*	Z *Z*	Z *Z*	Z *Z*
Poliphilus	*Garamond*	*Caslon*	*Baskerville*	*Didot*